D1065373

INTERIOR
PAINTING
Wallpapering
— and —
PANELING

A Beginner's Approach

INTERIOR PAINTING
Wallpapering  and
PANELING
A Beginner's Approach

GERSHON WHEELER

RESTON PUBLISHING COMPANY, INC., RESTON, VIRGINIA 22090

A Prentice-Hall Company

Library of Congress Cataloging in Publication Data

Wheeler, Gershon J
    Interior painting, wallpapering, and paneling.

  1. House painting—Amateurs' manuals. 2. Paper
-hanging—Amateurs' manuals. 3. Paneling—Amateurs'
manuals. I. Title.
TT323.W47   698   74-5135
ISBN 0-87909-363-3

© 1974 by
Reston Publishing Company, Inc.
A Prentice-Hall Company
Box 547
Reston, Virginia 22090

10 9 8 7 6 5 4 3 2

Printed in the United States of America

Acknowledgements

The author would like to thank the following for supplying information and photographs for this book:

> The Wallcovering Industry Bureau
> Wooster Brush Company
> PPG Industries
> Georgia-Pacific Corporation
> Masonite Corporation

Contents

Preface

A coat of paint, new wallpaper, and new wall panels not only improve the appearance of a home, they also increase the value. Yet many homeowners are afraid to tackle these jobs for fear of botching them. The purpose of this book is to show you how to do a professional job (and, incidentally, save a lot of money), when you paint, hang wall-coverings, or install new wall panels. Detailed explanations are included to enable you to perform these tasks easily with a minimum of expenditure for tools and equipment.

Gershon J. Wheeler

I

Painting

1

The Need for Paint

A coat of paint quickly brightens a dull room or a drab house. The improvement is immediately noticeable, even before the job is finished. Paint makes a home more attractive inside and out and thus creates a more pleasant environment. From a purely monetary consideration, a relatively inexpensive coat of paint adds value to the home far above the cost of the job.

The psychological value of paint is also important. By proper choice of colors a room can be made to seem warm or cool, exciting or comfortable, larger or smaller than it actually is.

The decorative value of paint, including its psychological aspects, is more or less taken for granted, but the most important reason for painting is *protection*. Wood and other building materials are affected by the elements, are attacked by insects and small animals, become corroded from moisture, and are even subject to damage from man-made pollutants in the atmosphere. Paint is the most economical protection against all these dangers.

The most obvious need for paint is as a protection from the elements. Sun, rain, snow, and wind all cause deterioration that can be prevented by a good coat of paint. The heat of the sun will dry out untreated wood so that the wood becomes brittle and cracks. Paint on the surface acts as an insulating layer, absorbing or reflecting the sun's energy and thus protecting the wood from drying. Rain and snow bring moisture to the surface where it is absorbed into the material, causing wood to rot or warp and causing iron to rust. A good coat of paint on the surface keeps the moisture out of the building material Wind whips up dust particles and blows them against a house, causing an abrasive action that actually wears away material. Paint is a protective coating that is better able to withstand this abrasion and that can be replaced whenever it does wear away. Note that paint on the surface protects the whole structure since most deterioration starts at the surface.

Heat and cold cause another problem. Materials generally expand with heat and shrink with cold; changes in temperature then cause variations that can loosen nails or cause splits in materials. The insulating value of paint helps maintain a more nearly constant temperature in the interior, and thus these variations are minimized.

Another source of damage to a home is man-made pollution. Chemicals in smoke and gases from auto exhausts and industry can cause serious damage to wood, metal, and other building materials. These pollutants occur almost everywhere in today's industrial society. But fortunately, a coat of paint is sufficient protection to keep them away from the surfaces of buildings.

Inside the house, paint is also important as a protective coating. If bathrooms where water vapor from baths and showers condenses on walls were without paint, walls and ceilings would be damaged quickly. Too much moisture can cause plaster walls and ceilings to disintegrate and can warp wood. In kitchens, paint is necessary to protect against moisture as well as against grease and cooking vapors, which can attack walls and ceilings in much the same way as pollutants do.

Paint is also important in protecting the inside of a home from normal wear. Paint or varnish on a floor prolongs the life of the surface. Without the coating, floors would quickly wear from ordinary traffic. Paint protects walls from greasy hands and scrapes from children's toys. If the paint wears, it can be replaced more easily and less expensively than a section of floor or wall.

Special paints are sometimes used for extra protection against specific dangers. Thus, fungicides and mildew preventatives are added to exterior paints. Fireproof paint is nonflammable and is used where there is a risk of fire. Although the material under the paint can burn, chemicals in the paint, when heated, release gases that form an insulating layer and tend to smother the flames.

In a strict sense, the word *paint* refers to an opaque coating applied to a surface. However, in general usage, any material that is applied with painting tools is commonly called "paint." This includes stains that penetrate as well as transparant surface coatings such as varnish and lacquer. All of these types of "paint" are discussed in Chapter 2.

2

Paints

The chemistry of paint is a continuously developing science; paints today bear little resemblance to those used a decade ago. Although the specific ingredients have been changed, there are four basic *types* of materials that go into paint. These are pigment, vehicle, thinner, and drier. Most paints have all four elements, although in some a single chemical may serve two functions. In transparent lacquer or varnish, there is no pigment; in fact, many paints lack one or more of the four basic elements. In special paints, other chemicals are added as mentioned in Chapter 1, to make the paint fireproof, to kill fungi, to prevent mildew, or for other specific requirements.

2.1 PIGMENTS

Pigment is the solid material that gives paint its color and hiding ability. Pigment is what is left on the surface as a hard coating when the paint has dried. Originally, pigments were natural substances, usually minerals, but occasionally derived from plants and animals. Most pigments today, however, are synthetic (man-made). The pigment is always ground to a dust-like powder before it is mixed in the paint.

The *coverage* of a paint is the area that can be covered with a given quantity, usually a gallon. Coverage is a function of the amount of pigment in the paint. Within broad limits, the more pigment, the greater the area that can be covered.

White pigments are usually used as a base in both white and colored paints. For colors other than white, a small amount of colored pigment is added. Most colored paints are white-based. Originally, the most common and most desirable pigment was *white lead*. White lead paint consists of white lead pigment in an oil vehicle. It was very popular until someone discovered that white lead is poisonous, and it quickly dropped from favor. A small amount of white lead (not enough to be dangerous) is still used with other pigments in some paints.

The most economical white pigment is *lithopone,* a synthetic material. It is quite satisfactory for interior painting, but is not able to withstand the elements as well as some other pigments. It is never used as the main pigment in outdoor paints, but is sometimes added in small quantities to other pigments in exterior paints to lower the cost.

Titanium oxide is a pigment that is a spinoff from the space age.

Titanium was a laboratory curiosity until uses were found for it in space flights and electronics. As a pigment, titanium oxide has much better hiding ability than white lead. However, since titanium oxide is more expensive, it is usually blended with other materials. For example, for exterior paints, calcium carbonate is mixed with the titanium oxide. As the paint ages, calcium carbonate forms a chalk-like dust on the painted surface. This "chalk" washes off in the rain, removing dirt with it, so that the surface appears clean and bright for the life of the paint job. Titanium oxide is also combined with small amounts of white lead and lithopone.

Colored pigments can be obtained from the earth; for example, from red clay. However, most colored pigments used today are synthetic. By controlling the manufacturing process, the manufacturers can reproduce the man-made colored pigments so that one batch of paint is precisely the same color as another. This is not always true of natural pigments.

2.2 EXTENDERS

Extenders are also solid materials in paints. Because they are solid, they are usually included in the broad class of pigments. However, they have practically no hiding ability and do not increase the coverage of the paint, as adding true pigment would do. Extenders do have specific uses and are not simply fillers.

One common extender is ordinary sand or *silica*. When paint dries with a hard slick surface, a second coat will not readily adhere to this surface. It is possible to roughen the first coat by rubbing it with sandpaper; but a simpler method is to mix a small amount of sand in the first coat as an extender. When the paint dries, the sand makes the surface rough enough to cause the next coat to adhere better. This roughness is called *tooth* and a small amount of tooth is desirable.

Too much sand makes the paint heavier and causes a reduction in coverage. When white lead paint was the most desirable, painters frequently judged a paint by its weight. The heavier the paint was, the more white lead it presumably contained, and therefore, the greater would be its coverage. Unfortunately, unscrupulous paint dealers sometimes added too much sand to make the paint heavy, since sand was much cheaper than white lead. As with all extenders, a small amount is useful, but too much spoils the paint. The percentage of extenders in the paint is indicated on the label; but if you don't know the proper limits, it is best to rely on reputable paint manufacturers. Bargain paints are usually no bargain.

Calcium carbonate, commonly called *whiting,* is another extender that causes chalking of exterior paints, as described in the preceding section. Again, only a small amount is necessary. Too much whiting will cause too rapid chalking so that the paint job looks streaked and wears out too rapidly. Chalking is desirable, but should not begin until a year or two after the paint has been applied. If chalking starts too soon, it is a sign that too much whiting was added to the paint.

Talc and *alumina* are very light powders. These are sometimes added to paints to help keep the heavier pigments in suspension. Other extenders reduce cracking and flaking and prevent other paint defects.

2.3 THINNERS

A liquid is sometimes added to paint to make it easier to apply. This is called a *thinner* or *solvent* because it thins the paint. The thinner evaporates as the paint dries. Thinners are usually added to the paint mixture at the time of its manufacture. For special methods of application, it may be necessary to add additional thinner. Oil-base paints use turpentine or mineral spirits as a thinner, and mineral spirits are also used to thin alkyd paints. Water-base paints are thinned with water. Kerosene, benzine, and other flammable thinners should be used with caution and stored carefully because of the danger of fire.

The same thinner may be used to clean up after a paint job is finished. Brushes, rollers, and other tools are cleaned in the thinner and then washed in soapy water.

2.4 DRIERS

Paints dry in three different ways, and a specific paint may use more than one method. Anything added to the paint to speed drying is called a *drier.*

Evaporation is one process of drying; to some extent, all paints dry by evaporation. However, some paints dry only by this method. Water-base paints dry by the evaporation of water. Shellac dries by the evaporation of the alcohol it contains. A paint that contains any volatile thinner also dries by evaporation.

A second drying process is *oxidation.* The oil in oil-base paints unites chemically with oxygen in the air to form a hard film. For this reason, oil in paint is sometimes called *drying oil.* Oil added to alkyd paints speeds drying in this fashion.

The third drying process is *polymerization*, a chemical combination of liquids to form a solid. This is the method of drying that occurs in epoxy paints and polyurethane coatings. The resulting coating is very hard and tough.

2.5 VEHICLES

If the pigment used in paint were just rubbed on a surface, it could not be applied evenly and would not adhere well. To facilitate spreading the paint easily and evenly, the pigments are ground into fine powder and stirred into a liquid. They do not dissolve in the liquid, but remain suspended, as in an emulsion (an *emulsion* is a mixture in which tiny particles are held in suspension in liquid). The liquid is called a *vehicle* or *carrier*. The vehicle may be a separate liquid from the thinner and drier used in the paint, or one liquid, such as water, may serve two or even all three functions. For this reason, it is customary to refer to the liquid part of paint as the vehicle, even though it may be a blend of vehicle, drier, and thinner.

At one time, oil was the only vehicle used. Oil is also a drier, as described in Section 2.4. Linseed oil was once preferred, but other vegetable and animal oils have recently been used, including castor oil, soybean oil, and fish oil. In modern oil-base paints, synthetic resins add strength to the paint, making the coating hard and tough.

Alkyd is a synthetic resin formed by combining an alcohol and an acid. Alkyd is combined with a drying oil and the combination is dissolved in a thinner to make a liquid that is used as the vehicle in alkyd paints.

Latex paints use a water emulsion as the vehicle. The emulsion in latex paint is a suspension of a synthetic resin in water. The first latex paint used butadiene-styrene (BDS) as a resin. Since BDS is a kind of artificial rubber called latex, the paint was called "latex paint." Some of the resins used are polyvinyl acetate (PVA), polyester, and acrylic. Latex paint can be thinned by adding water, and water is all that is needed to clean up afterward.

2.6 TYPES OF PAINT

When oil was the principal vehicle, paints were usually designated by the type of pigment used. *White lead* paint is an example of specifying a paint by its pigment. As different vehicles were developed, the characteristics of a paint depended more on the vehicle than the pigment. Thus, an oil-base paint with lithopone and an oil-base paint with titanium oxide have more in common than an oil-base paint and a latex paint, both of which use lithopone as a pigment. Consequently, paints are usually designated by their vehicles, even though there may be no trace of the vehicle after the paint dries. The three principal vehicles in paint are oil, alkyd, and latex.

Paint is also designated by its purpose. *House paint* is used on exteriors and is specially formulated to withstand the elements. *Floor paint* is a coating tough enough to withstand the abrasive action of foot traffic on floors and decks. *Marine paint* is an expensive, high-quality paint used on boats and formulated to withstand the effects of salt water and weather. *Masonry paint*, as its name implies, is designed to adhere better to masonry than ordinary paints.

In addition to vehicle and purpose, paint may be designated by its finish. *Flat paint* has a flat, lusterless finish. *Glossy paint* is shiny. The luster is achieved by adding special oils that dry to a shiny film on the surface. Glossy paints may be further separated into *high-gloss* paints and *semi-gloss* paints, depending on the degree of sheen. *Primers* or *primer-sealers* are used as a first coat on surfaces that will not take paint well. The primer is a material that will adhere to the surface, often sealing it, if it is porous, so that it will readily take a coat of regular paint. *Enamel* is a very hard finish and is used where resistance to abrasion, wear, or moisture is needed. Note that enamel and gloss paints are two different materials. Enamels usually have a glossy finish, but they are also available in flats.

A complete designation of a paint might include the vehicle, the purpose, and the finish. For example, *alkyd semi-gloss wall paint* is a complete designation. *Latex house paint* does not indicate the finish, but house paints are assumed to be flat unless otherwise specified. *Alkyd floor enamel* is an alkyd-base enamel and, since it is used on floors, it is usually glossy.

2.7 OIL-BASE PAINTS

At one time, oil-base paints were preferred and, in fact, almost the only paints used by professional painters. Oil-base house paint is still used occasionally for exteriors, but for interiors, they have been superseded by alkyd and latex paints.

Oil-base paints are available in flat, semi-gloss, and gloss finishes. This paint takes two to four days to dry and has a strong odor that persists even after it is completely dry. It dries by oxidation of the oil. The paint can be applied with a brush, roller, or other applicator, or a spray gun.

Oil-base paints have better hiding ability and greater coverage than latex. Also, oil-base paints can be applied to bare wood, metal, and plastic. These paints cannot be applied to damp walls.

Oil-base paints can be thinned with mineral spirits or turpentine. Surfaces to be painted can also be cleaned with these materials, and after the job is done, tools can be cleaned in the same thinner. Kerosene is a cheap solvent for oil-base paints and can be used for cleanup after the job is finished in place of mineral spirits or turpentine; but kerosene should not be used as a thinner in the paint itself. Kerosene is flammable and storage may be a problem.

Oil-base paint may still be available in paint stores, but it is rapidly becoming obsolete, even for outdoor work. Alkyd or latex paints are preferred for every type of paint job.

2.8 ALKYD PAINTS

The development of alkyd paints revolutionized the paint industry. Alkyd paints are superior to oil-base paints in so many respects that oil-base paints have been rendered obsolete. To be sure, some professional painters still use the older paints, but most have turned to the newer alkyds. Some of the advantages of alkyds over oil-base paints are:

1. Alkyd paints dry in 6 to 24 hours, as against 2 to 4 days for oil-base paints.

2. Alkyds are tougher and can stand more scrubbing and abrasion than oil-base paints.

3. Alkyds have very little objectionable odor, as oil-base paints do. **WARNING:** Although alkyd paints are odorless, their fumes are toxic and flammable until the paint dries. Adequate ventilation must be provided when painting with either alkyd or oil-base paint.

4. Alkyd paints last longer than oil-base paints.

5. The coverage of alkyd paint is excellent, and on porous masonry or dried wood, it is better than an oil-base paint.

6. Alkyd paints produce a tight paint film that is water-resistant. For bathroom walls and other areas where moisture may collect, alkyds are preferred.

Alkyd paints do have an oil base and can be thinned with mineral spirits just as oil-base paints can. Turpentine could also be used, but turpentine has a strong odor and should not be used in an "odorless" paint. Either turpentine or mineral spirits can be used to clean up after the job is finished. Kerosene may also be used to clean up the paint tools, but it is better to avoid flammable solvents.

Alkyd paints are available in flat, gloss, and semi-gloss finishes. So-called alkyd enamel may be high-gloss alkyd paint and not a true enamel. On interior woodwork, alkyd paints provide a tougher finish than latex. Some manufacturers provide both alkyds and latex paints in matching colors so that latex can be used on the walls and alkyd on the woodwork. This makes for an outstanding paint job, but it also makes more work, since different thinners are used for the two paints and two different methods of cleaning are necessary when the job is finished.

Alkyd paints are easy to apply by brush, roller, or spray gun. They do not show lap marks. These paints can be used directly on most surfaces without a primer. However, they cannot be applied to damp surfaces. Alkyds dry by oxidation of the drying oils in the paint.

2.9 LATEX PAINTS

Continuing the paint revolution started by the introduction of alkyd paints, the development of latex paints was a huge step forward. Latex threatens to make all other paints obsolete. Latex paint uses a vehicle consisting of an emulsion of a synthetic resin in *water*; because water is used as the solvent, latex paint has many advantages, some of which are:

1. Dries (by evaporation of water) in an hour or two, much faster than alkyds.
2. Can be applied easily by brush, roller, or spray gun without lap marks. Painting with latex takes less effort than painting with other paints.
3. Cleaning up after the job is finished is simple because tools can be cleaned in water rather than special thinners.
4. Is odorless and emits no dangerous fumes while drying.
5. Colors stay bright for years.
6. Can be applied on damp surfaces because water is part of the paint anyway. This means you can paint a house when there is morning dew on the wall or you can paint over new plaster.
7. Porous coating permits moisture below to evaporate. This prevents peeling and blistering.

8. Resists alkalis, which can damage alkyd paints. This makes latex excellent for masonry, which frequently contains alkali.
9. Can be applied directly to metals.
10. Withstands mildew.
11. Dries to a flexible surface that stretches or bends with movement of the surface below it.

Latex paints do have a few disadvantages:

1. They cannot be applied directly to new wood without a primer.
2. They do not adhere well to a high-gloss oil-base finish.
3. They cannot withstand scrubbing as well as alkyds.

Despite its disadvantages, latex paint is by far the "one best paint" for both interiors and exteriors. Development of latex paints is continuing, and the disadvantages are being minimized or eliminated.

Latex paint is available in flat, semi-gloss, and gloss finishes. There is also a *dripless* variety that has a much thicker consistency, which is supposed to be advantageous when painting ceilings. However, it is impossible to paint a ceiling without dripping, even with dripless paint, and the thicker paint is more expensive and requires more effort to apply than ordinary latex.

2.10 WATER-THINNED PAINTS

Latex paints are water-thinned, but the term *water-thinned paint* refers to materials that are not emulsions, including whitewash, calcimine, and casein paints. These are not really paints but *washes.* They are not durable and not easily washed without scrubbing off part of the coating. Water-thinned paints were used because they were inexpensive, were easy to apply, and dried quickly. They are seldom used today except where a quick inexpensive coating is needed.

Whitewash is a mixture of lime and water. *Calcimine* is a mixture of chalk and glue. Both are sold in powdered form; the user mixes the powder in water. *Casein paint* comes from skim milk. It is also sold as powder to be mixed with water as needed.

Portland cement paint is a special water-thinned mixture used on masonry. It is sold as a powder to be mixed with water. It is not really a paint since it doesn't dry, like a paint, but rather sets, like concrete. It is applied to damp masonry and must be kept moist for two or three days before it can be allowed to harden. Portland cement paint is cheap and forms a surface that will take any kind of paint. Colored pigments are sometimes added to it.

2.11 RUBBER-BASE PAINTS

Rubber-base paints, as indicated by the name, use a synthetic rubber as a base. The rubber is thinned in a volatile solvent such as naphtha or turpentine. These paints are tricky to apply because they dry very quickly. They were originally designed for use on concrete, stucco, brick, and other masonry surfaces and are most effective for abrasion resistance and waterproofing. Cleaning up rubber-base paints requires special solvents. For masonry, latex masonry paint has largely replaced these paints, but rubber-base paint is still used for painting swimming pools.

2.12 PRIMERS, SEALERS, AND UNDERCOATERS

Surfaces that have never been painted, such as bare wood, gypsum board, or metal, usually require more than one coat of paint. The first coat is called a *primer*, and all the coats together form what is called a *paint system*. The primer is usually a kind of paint different from that of the topcoat; it is used when the topcoat is a paint that cannot adhere well to the untreated surface. The primer must be compatible with both the surface to be painted and the top layer of paint. That is, the primer must adhere well to the surface, and when it has dried, the topcoat should adhere well to the primer. The primer must have *tooth*, or roughness, so that the finish coat can stick to it. In general, paint will not adhere to a surface that is too slick.

A primer is also used when the topcoat does not furnish satisfactory protection for the surface to be painted. For example, metal can rust even under a coating of paint. A protective primer to prevent rust is usually used on metal before the final coat of paint is applied.

Sometimes, defects or chemicals in a surface can mar a paint job. For example, resin from knotholes can "bleed through" the paint weeks or months after the finish is dry. In this case, a first coat of a special *sealer* is used to seal in any chemicals that can damage the finish. This is technically called a *primer-sealer* because it is a first coat. Sealers are also used to "seal" porous materials so that they do not absorb the moisture in the paint, which could cause imperfect drying.

Primer-sealers are used on bare wood that is to be coated with a clear finish.   Varnish, lacquer, and stains are absorbed into bare wood and raise a nap that is rough to the touch.   Sealers for this purpose are clear so that the natural grain of the wood will be visible.

When a new coat of paint is to be applied to a surface that has once been painted satisfactorily, no primer is required.   Of course, if the old paint job was poorly done, and especially if paint is peeling, exposing bare wood, it is best to proceed as though the surface had never been painted and to use a primer.   However, a surface that has once been painted has been sealed, if not by a primer, then by the paint itself. It may still be necessary to apply two coats, especially if a dark wall is to be covered with a light paint.   In this case, the first coat applied over the old paint is called an *undercoater;* it need not be of as high a quality as the finishing coat.   When the finish coat is an enamel or a gloss paint, the undercoat should be a flat paint because the finish coat will stick better to a flat than to a sleek coating.

Latex paint should never be applied directly to bare wood.   For best results, an alkyd primer should be used.   However, if you use alkyd for one coat and latex for another, you have two different cleanup jobs. It is not too bad if the alkyd paint is applied at one time and the latex at another, but it becomes a problem if you wish to put a primer on bare wood and at the same time put a latex coating somewhere else. The solution is to use a special latex primer that is available for exteriors.   This primer is somewhat different from ordinary latex paint in that it can be used on bare wood and takes about eight hours to dry, instead of the hour or two expected from conventional latex.   However, it is thinned with water, and water is used for cleaning up, as with other latex paints.

Similar considerations apply when the topcoat is to be an alkyd paint.   For some applications, latex may be a better primer, but for simplicity in cleaning up (this is said to be the worst part of a paint job), one should try to use one kind of paint for all coats.   An example of where latex is better for the first coat is on masonry.   Masonry frequently contains alkalis that can mar alkyd paint, but latex paint is resistant to damage from alkalis.   Again, there are alkyd primers available for covering masonry.

Metal that can rust should be painted with a rust-inhibiting primer before any other paint is applied.   The primer used on metals must make a good bond to the metal and also must insure a good bond to the finish coat.   Zinc chromate is an excellent primer for all metal because it prevents rust and also provides a coating that will take any other paint with a good bond.   However, zinc chromate is not available in a water-thinned vehicle.   There are latex metal primers available, which, though not as effective as zinc chromate, do have the advantages that go with latex paints.   Outdoors, all metal surfaces should have a primer applied before the finish coat. Inside the house, metal surfaces are less apt to rust and, therefore, need be primed only if the paint to be used will not stick well. Latex paint can be applied to bare metal inside the house, and usually one coat is sufficient.

Plaster and gypsum board will not take alkyd paints, but latex adheres nicely to either. However, because of the porosity of both of these materials and the likelihood of raising the nap on gypsum board, the first coat is more difficult to apply and gives less coverage than subsequent coats. The best primer is a latex primer-sealer that is really only a thin latex paint. Because of its thinness, it goes on easily and seals the pores in the material. One coat of ordinary latex paint over the primer completes the job. Like ordinary latex, this interior latex primer dries quickly.

2.13 CLEAR FINISHES

Clear finishes contain no pigment and thus have no "hiding" ability as paints do. They are generally used to finish surfaces so that the natural grain is visible and are sometimes called *natural finishes.* Although some of these natural finishes are hard and tough enough to withstand abrasion that would quickly wear paint, they do not wear as well when exposed to sun and extremes of heat and cold. The pigment in paint is a protection against the elements that is missing in clear finishes.

Shellac is a clear finish made by dissolving an insect resin, *lac,* in alcohol. It dries in about 15 minutes and forms a hard coating that can seal plaster or gypsum board and prevent resins, alkalis, and other impurities from bleeding through the surface. For these reasons, shellac is an excellent primer-sealer for most other paints. It is also used as a clear finish on floors and furniture, but must be protected with a wax coating. Shellac can be applied by brush or spray gun.

Shellac is usually packaged in a *four-pound* or *five-pound cut.* The cut refers to the amount of resin dissolved in one gallon of alcohol. It should always be thinned to something between a two-pound and three-pound cut before being used. Ask your paint dealer how much alcohol to add to the cut you buy to get a 2½-pound cut. The exact cut doesn't matter, but two thin coats of shellac give a longer-lasting finish than one thick coat. For small quantities, the dealer will usually sell you shellac that is already thinned.

Old shellac does not dry well. Look for a date on the package and try not to buy shellac more than six months old. If the can is undated, ask to try a small amount on a scrap of wood. It should get tacky in a few minutes. Because shellac ages, don't buy more than you need at one time.

Shellac is available in two types: orange and white. Orange is cheaper and is a good primer under opaque finishes. White shellac should be used when a clear finish is desired. Because shellac is thinned with alcohol, denatured alcohol is also used for cleaning brushes and other equipment when the job is finished. For the same reason, shellac should not be used to finish tables or bars where alcoholic drinks may be spilled. A shellac finish also gets cloudy when water is spilled on it. However, on furniture that is not subject to spilled beverages, shellac makes a nice looking, inexpensive finish.

Lacquer is a clear finish that dries very rapidly and can be applied only with a spray gun. Special slower drying lacquers are available for brushing, but they are inferior to the fast drying variety. Lacquer consists of nitrocellulose dissolved in a volatile solvent and is thinned with a special mixture of solvents called *lacquer thinner*. The same mixture is used to clean the spray gun after the job is done. Lacquer acts as a paint remover, so it cannot be applied over old paint coating. However, it can be used over shellac. Lacquer is tricky to apply, and considerable practice is required before it can be put down correctly. It is also highly flammable. For these reasons, the home handyman should probably avoid using lacquer.

Varnish is a mixture of resin, oil, thinner, and dryer. The proportions and types of ingredients can be varied to design the best varnish for a particular application. No one varnish can be used for every purpose. A stiff brush should be used, and this brush should not be used for anything else, since even a small amount of pigment from another job can spoil a varnish finish. Varnish can also be applied with a lint-free cloth pad. Varnish must not be stirred, because stirring causes bubbles that cannot be brushed out. In fact, the formation of bubbles is the only problem that arises when varnish is applied. Tools can be cleaned in turpentine or mineral spirits.

When varnish dries, the solvent evaporates, first, then the drying oils oxidize. Drying normally takes about 24 hours. The dry coating is clear, hard, and long-lasting. By proper choice of synthetic resins and oils the coating can be made to withstand water, alcohol, most solvents, high or low temperatures, and severe abrasion. Different types of varnish are used for different applications.

Floor varnish is formulated to withstand the heavy abrasion of foot traffic and scraping of furniture across the floor. It can be scrubbed. clean with soap and water and can be waxed. No other varnish produces as hard a finish. Floor varnish dries more rapidly than other varieties, usually taking 12 to 16 hours.

Cabinet-finishing varnish is a clear material that dries to a hard coat that can be polished to a high gloss. It dries in 24 hours.

Spar varnish is a very expensive variety designed for exterior and marine use. It will withstand the elements and wide variations in temperature. It is not used inside the house, however, because it cannot stand abrasion as well as floor varnish and cannot be polished to as fine a sheen as cabinet-finishing varnish.

There are many other types of varnish available in finishes ranging from a dull flat to an extra high gloss. The drying time, too, varies from two hours to two days. An old rule of thumb says that the shorter the drying time, the poorer the varnish, but with the development of synthetic resins, this rule has many exceptions. To avoid inferior products, buy from reliable dealers.

Penetrating floor sealer is a type of varnish that penetrates the wood and seals it with a thin hard coating. It is not as tough as ordinary floor varnish, but scratches on the penetrating floor sealer do not stand out so much as scratches on floor varnish.

2.14 STAINS

A wood *stain* is used to darken or color a wood without hiding the wood's natural grain and texture. It is important to note that a stain is not a protective finish, and a clear finish — such as one of those discussed in the preceding section — is needed to protect the surface. Stains are made of colored dyes dissolved in solvents and are usually classified according to their solvents.

Stains are absorbed by the wood and, therefore, must be applied only to bare wood. The stain is usually brushed on freely, but it may also be wiped on with cloth. The excess is wiped off with a cloth after the stain has been allowed to soak into the wood for 5 to 15 minutes. The stain should be allowed to dry 24 hours before further treatment.

Oil stains use turpentine or naphtha as the solvent in an oil vehicle. These stains are used mainly on exteriors. The oil penetrates so that the wood is colored not only on the surface, but also to an appreciable depth. For this reason, stain doesn't have to be renewed as often as paint, even if the wood wears.

Oil stains may be clear or pigmented. The pigmented type has a small amount of pigment added, which partially obscures the grain of the wood. However, like the clear stains, the pigmented type soaks into the wood and, in this respect, is different from paint that simply covers the surface.

Water stains employ water as a vehicle and penetrate deeply, much more so than other stains. They are difficult to apply because they start to penetrate immediately and may do so unevenly, causing the surface to look streaked. Water causes the grain to rise so that more sanding is needed than with other stains.

Alcohol stains use alcohol or acetone as a vehicle. They are the fastest drying and, consequently, the most difficult stains to work with. They are used mainly under lacquers. The home handyman should avoid using either water or alcohol stains since considerable practice is required to master the proper application of these materials.

Non-grain-raising stains use a special solvent that does not raise the grain of the wood as it is applied. These stains do not penetrate as far as other stains, but they do not bleed through protective coatings and they do not fade. Because the grain is not raised, sanding is not necessary after using this type of stain. This stain is usually applied by spraying, but it can be wiped or brushed on as well.

A *varnish stain* is a combination of a stain and a varnish. It accomplishes two operations in one step. The wood is stained and a varnish coating is applied at the same time. It is cheap and fast, but it is neither attractive nor long-lasting.

After wood has been stained, a *filler* is applied to fill the pores of wood. Fillers come in two forms, liquid and paste. Liquid fillers do not fill as well as the pastes and thus are used only on close-grained woods. Paste fillers are usually thinned with turpentine and may be used on any type of wood. Close-grained woods include pine, fir, maple, and birch; open-grained woods include oak, walnut, ash, and mahogany.

The filler is usually brushed on after the wood is stained. As it dries, it becomes duller, and when this happens (about 15 minutes after application), the excess is wiped off with a clean rag. The surface is then ready for finishing. On close-grained woods having little porosity, shellac can also be used as a filler.

2.15 ENAMEL

Enamel is a special kind of pigmented paint that uses varnish added to the vehicle and dries to a smooth coating that combines the durability of varnish with the beauty of a pigmented finish. In popular jargon, the term "enamel" is applied to any gloss paint, but the gloss paints do not have the wearing qualities of enamels. Enamel is available in flat finishes as well as a variety of glossy finishes. The amount of gloss in the finish is controlled by the ratio of pigment to oil in the mixture.   The more oil there is, the shinier will be the surface finish.

Just as there are many types of varnish, so also there are many types of enamel, depending on the varnish used and the vehicle. Alkyd enamel and latex enamel are the two broad classes that depend on the vehicle.   Latex enamel is not so durable as alkyds but does have the advantage of all latex paints: cleanup in water.   Enamels are made for special purposes and are designated as *floor enamel, implement enamel* (for farm implements), *exterior enamel, automobile enamel,* etc.   For best results, an undercoater is necessary with enamel.   The undercoater is usually a white finish and may be flat, but if a high-gloss final finish is required, the undercoat should have a gloss finish.   The most important requirement of the undercoater is that it form a tight surface film so that the final enamel finish will not penetrate it.   Ordinary paint could be used as an undercoater, but to ensure the tight film, it is best to use the enamel undercoater specified for the final enamel finish.   This is usually indicated on the label of the can of enamel.   Enamel is generally applied with a brush and dries rapidly.

3

Tools and Equipment

3.1 BRUSH FILAMENTS

Paintbrushes were used by primitive man and are among the oldest of man's tools. Early brushes were made of reeds or stems of large leaves shredded into thin fibers. Later, animal hair proved superior for brush filaments; the best was *bristle*, the hair of the hog. The word "bristle" is frequently, but erroneously, applied to all bristle-like material, and it is common to find reference to "nylon bristles" or "horsehair bristles." However, the Federal Trade Commission of the United States insists that brushes labeled "pure bristle" be 100 percent hog hair and that brushes with mixed filaments have the ingredients listed in descending order of percentages. Thus, a brush stamped "bristle and horsehair" should have more bristle than horsehair.

The *filaments* or *hairs* of modern paint brushes are classified as either *natural* or *synthetic*. Natural filaments come from animals; vegetable fibers are no longer used. Although the best natural filaments are bristles, horsehair is also used because it is cheaper, but horsehair is markedly inferior to bristle for paint brushes. Some manufacturers put out a line with mixed filaments, bristles on the outside and horsehair in the center, to combine the economy of horsehair with the performance of bristle. Brushes with mixed natural filaments are superior to plain horsehair brushes, but not as good as pure bristle.

Synthetic or man-made filaments are in a state of continued development. The early synthetic brushes used *nylon* filaments and were inferior to bristle brushes. However, improved nylon and other newer synthetics are as good as bristle for most applications and far better than bristle when used with latex paints. Natural bristles absorb water and thus lose their stiffness and elasticity in water-base paints. Nylon filaments also absorb a small amount of water, but not enough to affect their painting performance. Newer synthetics like *polyester* absorb almost no water. Diehards who insist that synthetics can never replace natural bristles are the same people who insisted that latex paint would never supplant oil paint.

Paintbrushes must be capable of picking up a large amount of paint and carrying it with a minimum of dripping. This paint-holding ability is brought about first by *flags* at the tips of the filaments. A flag is simply a split end; hog bristles, which have these flags naturally, are excellent paint carriers. However, as a paint brush is used, the flags wear down, leaving long *tapered points* on the tips of the bristles.

Bristles still hold paint because of capillary action between the tapered points and because of their rough surface. This roughness extends the full length of the bristle and allows a brush to be used after considerable wear. Horsehair filaments are not split naturally, but manufacturers of brushes sometimes split the ends of horsehairs to make flags and thereby improve the brush. However, horsehair lacks the roughness necessary after the flags wear off.

The first nylon brushes used smooth filaments with split ends, but these were not as satisfactory as bristle brushes. Subsequently, the nylon filaments were roughened in manufacture and, as a result, modern nylon brushes give excellent performance. Manufacturers mix long and short, as well as flagged and pointed, filaments to get improved painting action. The tips of some nylon filaments are shown magnified in Fig. 3–1, illustrating flags and points.

Filaments must be *resilient*. That is, when bent and released, they should resume their shape. This elasticity is achieved by tapering the filament from its base to its tip. Hog bristles have this taper naturally, but horsehair does not. This is another reason why horsehair filaments are inferior. Synthetic filaments are manufactured with tapers and have superior resilience.

Most paintbrushes have black filaments only because consumers seem to prefer black to any other color. However, natural bristles come in many colors, and synthetics can also be made in all colors. To make filaments black, either natural or synthetic, they must be

FIGURE 3–1. Nylon Filaments. Photo Courtesy of Wooster Brush Company.

colored with an excellent grade of black dye, which increases the cost of a brush. Cheap dyes could run and ruin a paint job.

Although bristles have natural characteristics that make them especially suitable for paintbrushes, manufacturers have developed synthetic filaments with flags, rough surfaces, tapers, and points so that the synthetic brushes are at least equal to the best natural brushes. Moreover, bristles do vary in quality, whereas the quality control in the manufacture of synthetic filaments is excellent.

Natural filaments such as hog bristles or horsehair tend to wilt in water. Therefore, they should not be used with latex or other water-base paints. Nylon brushes were a necessary invention when latex paints were developed. The early nylon brushes, as well as the cheaper ones still available, work well with latex but deteriorate in oil-base paints. However, good nylon filaments and other synthetics manu-factured today can be used with oil-base, alkyds, and latex without deterioration.

The construction of a brush is illustrated in the cross-sectional view of Fig. 3–2. The filaments are attached to a wooden or plastic handle by means of a metal ferrule that holds them firmly in place. The part of the filaments next to the handle is called the *heel* of the brush. Shown in the photograph are spacer plugs in the heel, which give the brush a taper and allow it to hold more paint. Some manu-facturers achieve a taper in cheap brushes by omitting filaments in the center of the clump so that the brush is "hollow." Such a brush is difficult to use because it does not release paint evenly.

The *formulation* of a brush is the blend of filaments of different

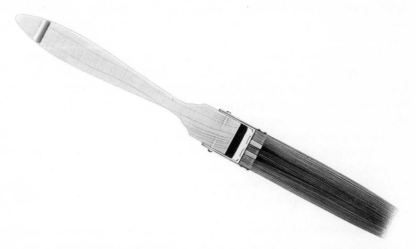

FIGURE 3–2. Brush Construction. Photo Courtesy of Wooster Brush Company.

lengths and sometimes of different types to achieve the best painting action.   Some manufacturers insist that their formulations are best and keep them closely guarded secrets.   However, many manufacturers make excellent brushes, and although the proper blend of long and short filaments is important, it is not a mysterious process.   In good brushes, filaments are selected to give the right amount of stiffness and flexibility while preserving maximum paint-carrying ability.

3.2 HOW TO SELECT A BRUSH

Don't buy a cheap brush!   A good brush is expensive, but it is a good investment.   A cheap brush is more difficult to use and does not give as good a paint job.   A good brush carries more paint than a cheap brush and does not drip as much paint.   You will be able to paint more rapidly with a good brush because it applies the paint evenly without brush marks.   Cheap brushes wear out rapidly or become unmanageable because of "wild" bristles, but a good brush will last a lifetime.   In fact, some manufacturers offer nylon brushes with a lifetime guarantee.

Excellent brushes are available with either natural or synthetic filaments.   You should buy synthetic brushes because these are superior for use with latex paints.   Synthetic brushes are also easier to clean when the painting is finished.   The most common synthetic material in brushes is nylon, which is quite satisfactory.   Polyester is somewhat better, and undoubtedly newer synthetics will be developed with improved performances.   However, although the professional painter can detect differences, any good synthetic brush will suit the average homeowner who paints only occasionally.

Make sure the brush is *full*.   That is, it should not be hollow in the center.   The filaments should be held tightly by a ferrule that is fastened securely to the handle.   The ferrule itself should be made of stainless steel or some other metal that will not rust when used with the new water-base paints.

The handle should be made of wood or plastic; plastic is preferred since it is not affected by water.   Even if you will use the brush for oil-base paints, you should choose a plastic handle because you will wash the brush in water when you are finished.   The only requirement on shape and size of the handle is: Does it feel comfortable when you hold it?

Filaments should be tapered and have *flags*, or split tips.   The taper makes the brush flexible and elastic.   Press the brush against the palm of your hand or a smooth surface and observe how the filaments behave.   First, they should not fan out at random, but should remain in a more or less compact cluster. This is an important consideration when you are painting in corners or on trim, where wildly spreading filaments can apply paint to the wrong areas. The filaments should flex more at the tip, where they are narrower, than at the base. If filaments bend at the base, but are more or less straight, they lack the necessary flexibility to apply paint smoothly and evenly. Now release the filaments. They should spring back to their former position. Beware of brushes with filaments so soft that they feel silky and do not return when released or filaments so hard that they feel hard and sharp against the palm of your hand.

The proper length of filament depends on the size of the brush. A single filament is flexible, but when many filaments are bound together, the flexibility varies with lengths of filament and the number bound together. Typically, a good 4-inch brush has filaments about 4 inches long, as shown in Fig. 3–4. Wider brushes like the 6-inch brush in Fig. 3–3 also have filaments about 4 inches long. Narrower brushes, like the 2-inch brush in Fig. 3–5, have filaments longer than the width of the brush.

If you have any doubts about choosing a brush, ask your dealer to make a recommendation. Any high-quality synthetic brush made by a reputable manufacturer should be quite acceptable. Let your paint

FIGURE 3–3. Six-inch Brush.   **FIGURE 3–4.** Four-inch Brush.   **FIGURE 3–5.** Two-inch Brush.

Photos Courtesy of PPG Industries.

dealer be your guide if you are not aware of the leading manufacturers of paintbrushes.

For painting large surfaces, you may use a *wall brush* or a roller. Wall brushes range from 3 to 6 inches in width, and if you decide to use a brush rather than a roller, you should buy the largest that you can handle comfortably. The bigger the brush, the faster the job will be, since you cover more area with each stroke. However, this is true only if your arm doesn't tire from wielding a large brush heavy with paint. The 6-inch model in Fig. 3–3 is too big for the occasional painter, and most homeowners find a 4-inch brush, like that shown in Fig. 3–4, a convenient size to use.

Whether you use a brush or a roller for large areas, you will need a smaller brush for painting trim, woodwork, and small areas. If you use a roller, you need a small brush for cutting into corners that cannot be covered with a roller, such as at the junction of walls and ceiling. Small brushes are called *trim* or *sash brushes.* Nominally, sash brushes are smaller than trim brushes, but because one brush can be used for both sashes and trim, some manufacturers lump them under the name *sash-and-trim brushes.* Sash brushes run from about ½ to 1½ inches in width, and trim brushes from 1 to 2 inches. Trim brushes are small versions of the larger wall brushes, but sash brushes may have round or oval cross sections as well as rectangular. These are shown in Fig. 3–6; the flat trim brush in Fig. 3–6(a) is similar to the two-inch brush of Fig. 3–5. The cross section is rectangular, and the filaments are cut square. The oval sash brush in Fig. 3–6(b) usually comes with a round handle so that you hold it as you do a pencil. The angled sash brush in Fig. 3–6(c) has a rectangular cross section, but the filaments are cut at an angle. This enables you to paint window sashes without having your hand bumping the glass.

A *varnish brush* is a special brush for applying varnish or enamel. It is illustrated in Fig. 3–7. This brush has a chisel edge as shown in the edge view in Fig. 3.7(b). The filaments are longer and softer than those in a trim brush. The chisel edge enables you to apply paint or varnish in corners or on furniture or trim without accidently touching surfaces that are not to be painted.

If you were a professional painter, you would want a wide variety of brushes for different purposes; but for the occasional paint job, you can get by with a wall brush or a roller for larger areas and one small brush. It's not illegal to use a varnish brush for painting trim or a trim brush for varnish. Whether you use an angled sash brush or a flat or oval brush is a matter of personal preference.

A trim brush without bristles is also available, illustrated in Fig. 3–8. This is made of plastic sponge and looks and feels like a paint

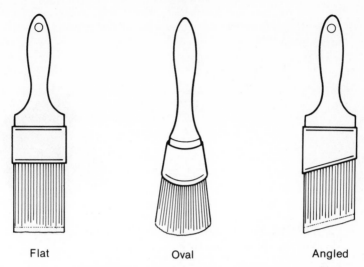

Flat   Oval   Angled

FIGURE 3–6. Sash and Trim Brushes.

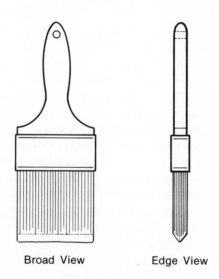

Broad View   Edge View

FIGURE 3–7. Varnish Brush.

brush. Originally, plastic sponge brushes were designed as disposable brushes to be used once and thrown away, but with improved plastics, these brushes are now cleanable and reusable. They apply a smooth finish without brush marks. Note the chisel edge that permits painting sharp, straight edges. A plastic sponge brush can be used with

FIGURE 3–8. Plastic Sponge Brush. Photo Courtesy of
Wooster Brush Company.

varnish, enamel, latex, alkyd or oil-base paint. It should *not* be used
with lacquer or shellac.

3.3 HOW TO USE A BRUSH

During painting and cleaning and especially when painting is interrupted, it is necessary to hang a brush in a solvent with the tip off the
bottom of the container. The simplest way to do this is to pass a wire,
such as may be cut from a metal coat hanger, through a hole in the
brush as shown in Fig. 3–9. With the wire in place, the tip of the brush
should be about an inch from the bottom of the can. A suitable container for solvent is a large coffee can or fruit juice can or an inexpensive paint bucket. Most brushes have holes in their handles, as is
evident in Figs. 3–3, 3–4, and 3–5, but these holes are not always located in the right place for the container you have on hand. The first
thing to do with a new brush then is to drill a hole in the handle at a
suitable location for supporting it in the can.

Before you paint with a new brush, you should clean and prepare
it for the job. Tap the brush vigorously against the palm of your hand
and snap the filaments against your fingers to shake out loose filaments and dust. If the brush has natural bristles, it should be suspended in a can of linseed oil for at least 12 hours. This softens the
bristles so that the brush holds more paint. After removing the brush
from the linseed oil, squeeze out excess oil and swish the brush in
turpentine. However, linseed oil is not compatible with shellac or
lacquer, and therefore, if you are going to use your brush with these
materials, you should skip the linseed oil preconditioning. Note that

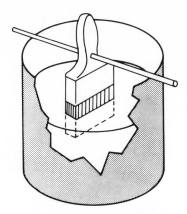

FIGURE 3-9. Wire to Support Brush.

the linseed oil bath is a one-time event. After the bristles have absorbed the oil, they will not need conditioning again. If you are going to use the brush with alkyd paint, you can omit the turpentine wash. For use with latex paint, wash out the turpentine with soap and warm water, then rinse.

If the new brush is a synthetic such as nylon or polyester, it doesn't need preconditioning. You may want to wash the filaments in warm water and mild soap to make sure that all traces of dirt and oil are removed. The brush is now ready for painting. If you are using latex paint, you don't have to wait for the brush to dry out. Occasionally, a new brush will have one or two filaments that are "wild," that is, filaments that do not lie parallel to the rest. Simply cut them off with a sharp knife.

Hold the brush in any way that feels comfortable. You may find that you can control small brushes more easily by holding them with your fingers like you hold a pencil. For large surfaces where delicate control is not needed, it may be less tiring to hold the brush in your fist.

Do not overload the brush. Too much paint in the brush tends to drip and splash on application and leaves too thick a film on the surface. To avoid this, dip the brush in the paint to only half the filament length. Then remove excess paint by tapping the brush lightly against the inside of the container. Do not drag the brush across the rim of the can, since that tends to make the filaments bunch together. Never stir paint with your brush.

Try to avoid getting paint in the heel of the brush. This is the most difficult part of the brush to clean, and if any paint remains and hardens in the heel, the effect is to shorten the flexible part of the bristles and make painting more difficult.

Paint should be applied with short strokes and then smoothed out with longer ones. Don't use too much pressure. Lift the brush at the end of each stroke before reversing direction. Never paint edge-on. This curls the brush. For smaller areas, use a smaller brush. Don't use a large brush to paint pipes and other objects that are thin compared to the width of the brush. Don't jab the brush into corners. The emphasis should be on letting the brush do the work. Let the paint flow on the surface instead of forcing it.

For smoother finishes, go over the surface lightly with the brush unloaded after every three or four brushfulls. The smoothing strokes with the brush almost dry should be at right angles to the direction of the first strokes.

If a loose filament from the brush is deposited on the freshly painted surface, you can usually pick it up with the brush by dabbing at it lightly. After removing the filament, brush lightly over the area to cover the marks.

Interruptions pose a problem. If you stop for a short time, you may suspend the brush in the paint bucket, making sure that the filaments are not immersed more than half their length and that they do not touch the bottom of the container. The brush should not be left in paint for more than an hour. For very short interruptions, such as to answer the telephone, it is all right to lay the brush flat on a pile of newspapers. However, if you are using latex paint, you must realize that it dries quickly, and you must not leave the brush exposed to the air for more than a minute or two. You can wrap the brush in a damp cloth and lay it flat; then it will not dry out as long as the cloth remains moist. For longer interruptions, as for a lunch hour, you can wrap the brush in a double thickness of aluminum foil or in transparent plastic wrap to keep it from drying out.

If your paint job takes more than a day, so that it is necessary to store the brushes overnight, your best procedures depend on the type of paint you are using. With latex paint, cleaning is simple, and you should clean out the paint from the brush with soap and water. Lay the clean brush on a flat surface. It is not necessary to wrap it or dry it. With alkyds or oil-base paints, you can suspend the brush in linseed oil or turpentine overnight. The thinner should cover the filaments completely. When you are ready to paint again, wipe out excess thinner and rub the brush over newspaper until it seems dry.

3.4 HOW TO CARE FOR A BRUSH

If you take proper care of a good brush, it will literally last a lifetime. Some manufacturers even go so far as to guarantee their top-quality brushes "for your lifetime, if cleaned and maintained according to our instructions." Yet despite the fact that these instructions are included in the package with every brush, they are frequently ignored.

The most important part of maintenance is proper cleaning. This is not a difficult task, but it isn't very interesting and thus is frequently rushed and incomplete. Make sure every bit of paint is removed from the brush before you store it.

To clean a brush, soak it in thinner or solvent for a few minutes. Make sure the thinner works up into the heel of the brush; then wash out the thinner with water and mild soap. That's all there is to it, but you must be thorough. To ensure that the thinner gets into all parts of the brush, especially the heel, work it in with your fingers. You may want to wear rubber gloves if you are using turpentine or other solvents that can dissolve the oils in your skin. Agitate the brush in the thinner so that every filament is separately exposed to the solution. The procedure varies slightly with the kind of paint used.

After painting with latex or other water-base paints, rinse out most of the paint under a water faucet. Work the filaments with your fingers to get out as much as possible, especially around the heel of the brush. Mix a solution of mild soap and warm water and soak the brush in it, again working the filaments to get the soapy water well into the heel. Rinse several times in clean warm water or under a warm water faucet until all paint is removed.

After using alkyds or other oil-base paints, soak the brush in kerosene and agitate it to get the solvent into all parts of the brush. Repeat until the brush shows no trace of paint. Wash in soap and warm water until there is no sign of color in the wash. Then rinse in clear water.

For other finishes, use the appropriate thinner or solvent specified by the manufacturer. Always follow with a soapy water bath to wash out the thinners and a clear rinse to remove the soap.

When the brush is clean and still damp from the water rinse, comb out the filaments with a brush comb. This consists of a wooden or metal handle with metal pins or teeth, as illustrated in Fig. 3-10. Combing straightens interior filaments that might be matted and keeps the brush in proper shape.

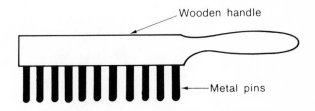

FIGURE 3-10. Comb for Brushes.

Hang the brush up to dry with filaments pointing down. When dry, wrap in foil or plastic wrap to keep out dirt, and store flat.

Do not use hot water on natural bristles. As a precaution, when the directions above specify warm water, use cold water on natural bristles, but warm or hot water can be used on nylon or other synthetic brushes. Some synthetics cannot be soaked in alcohol or lacquer thinner. When you buy your brush, find out whether it can be used in shellac, lacquer, and their solvents. Ammonia can be used in place of alcohol as a solvent for shellac.

Outside of proper cleaning, maintenance consists chiefly of avoiding improper use. Some of the common offenses are mentioned in the preceding section, and repeated bad practice can lead to the troubles illustrated in Fig. 3–11.

Wild filaments, illustrated in Fig. 3–11(a), are the result of improper cleaning and failure to comb out the brush when done. The fishtail in Fig. 3–11(b) is caused by painting a pipe or other thin structure with a brush too wide for the job. Fingers, shown in Fig. 3–11(c), are usually the result of using the brush edge-on instead of painting with the broad side. Fingering can also be caused by drawing the brush frequently across the rim of the paint container. Curl in Fig. 3–11(d) is caused by letting the brush rest with its filaments in contact with the bottom of the container. Other troubles are the result of improper cleaning, leaving paint in the heel of the brush, or neglecting to clean a brush so that it dries to a solid, hard lump.

If you have brushes that have been damaged by neglect or misuse, don't throw them away. It is usually possible to get a good brush back into shape as long as the filaments are still firmly attached to the

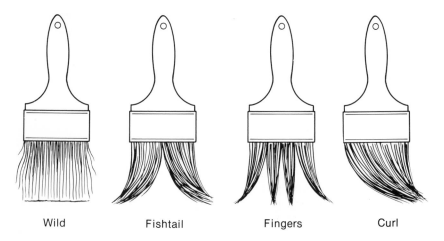

Wild   Fishtail   Fingers   Curl

FIGURE 3–11. Neglected Brushes.

handle. The treatment consists of two parts: (1) removing all traces of paint and (2) shaping the brush. If paint has dried in a brush, it must be removed before the brush can be reshaped. The troubles depicted in Fig. 3–11 can be accompanied by dried paint in the brush or they may occur even when all paint is removed by careful cleaning after each use.

If the brush is a solid mass of dried paint or if it has a lot of paint dried in the heel, it should be soaked in a chemical paint cleaner, which is stronger than most paint thinners. Hang the brush in a container so that the tip does not touch the bottom and pour in enough cleaner to cover the filaments completely. It is even better if you cover the ferrule. For a heeled-up brush, a few hours soaking may be enough; but if the brush is completely solid with paint, you may have to let it soak for a week. It is better to buy a mild cleaner that takes longer since it is less likely to do damage if you soak the brush too long. After soaking, the paint should be softened to a jelly or may be completely dissolved. Comb out any loose paint with an old comb and then wash the brush in hot, soapy water. (Bristle brushes cannot stand hot water and so must be washed in cold water and strong soap or detergent.) Repeat, if necessary, until the bristles are soft and flexible, as in a new brush.

Even after all traces of old paint are removed from the brush, it may still be misshapen, as in Fig. 3–11. If this is the case, suspend the brush in linseed oil for about an hour and then comb it as straight as possible with the brush comb shown in Fig. 3–10. Combing straightens interior filaments that might be matted. Dip the brush in linseed oil again and, while it is still wet, shape it and wrap it tightly in aluminum foil to maintain the shape. Store it flat for at least two days. Then clean out the oil with turpentine and wash the brush in warm, soapy water to remove the turpentine. Rinse in clear water and comb the brush once more. Hang to dry and then wrap in plastic wrap or foil for storage.

3.5 TYPES OF ROLLERS

For painting large, flat surfaces, paint rollers are easier and faster to work with than brushes. Like brushes, rollers come in a wide variety of styles, sizes, and materials. Also like brushes, prices of rollers cover a wide range, depending on material and quality of workmanship.

The *cover* of a roller is shown in Fig. 3–12. Covers may be made of a synthetic material, such as nylon or rayon, or of a natural fiber, such as wool or mohair. Natural fibers should not be used with latex or other water-base paints, but mohair provides the smoothest finish for applying enamel. The rayon rollers are cheap and generally not

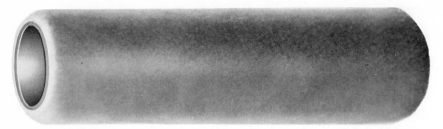

FIGURE 3–12. Roller Cover. Photo Courtesy of Wooster Brush Company.

worth the money. Good quality nylon rollers can be used with any kind of paint.

The *core* of the cover, the inner tube, may be made of laminated cardboard, metal, or plastic. The only important consideration is that the core retain its shape after having been washed in thinner and water. Cardboard tubes are cheap, but do not last as long as metal or plastic cores. If the core is metal, it should be rust-proof since it will be used in water-base paints and will be washed in water.

The *nap* on the roller may vary in length from about ¼-inch to well over an inch. The shorter the nap, the smoother the coating you can apply. For most smooth paint jobs, use a roller with a ¼-inch nap. For slightly rougher surfaces like plaster or gypsum board, a ⅜-inch nap is better. You rarely need anything longer than this for indoor painting. The ¾-inch nap is usually used for outdoor finishes on rougher surfaces like stucco, rough plaster, and rough wood. Naps longer than this may be used on rough masonry and chain-link fences.

Rollers vary in length from about three to 18 inches. The larger the roller, the greater the surface you can paint with each stroke; but larger rollers may be awkward to handle and require oversized pans to hold the paint. For most indoor painting, a nine-inch roller is preferred.

The roller cover slips onto a frame, as is shown in Fig. 3–13. An assembled roller is shown in Fig. 3–14. The roller part of the frame should rotate easily, but should not spin too fast, or the roller will spatter paint. You should be able to attach the cover to the frame quickly and easily so that you can simply change covers when you want to use a different paint. The handle should be made of plastic or other material that can be washed in water. For painting ceilings without a ladder, it is desirable to have a roller with an extension handle. The extension screws into a threaded socket in the handle of the frame.

Rollers are used with a paint pan that has a sloping bottom. Pans vary in width to accommodate rollers of different sizes, and the most

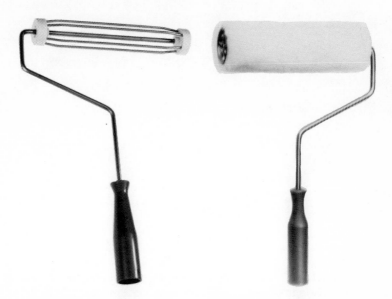

FIGURE 3–13. Roller Frame.   **FIGURE 3–14.** Assembled Roller.
Photos Courtesy of Wooster Brush Company

common, shown in Fig. 3–15, is designed for a 9-inch roller.   Legs at
the shallow end of the pan keep it from tipping and also keep the upper
end of the ramp out of the paint.   Pans are also available with clamps
to fasten onto an extension ladder for outdoor painting.

When a roller is used at junctions of walls and ceiling, it cannot always reach every spot.   This is shown in Fig. 3–16.   In Fig. 3–16(a), the
roller is shown in a corner at the junction of two walls and a ceiling.
The roller cannot touch the corner.   As shown in Fig. 3–16(b) and (c),
the roller can be positioned to reach all parts of a junction of two surfaces.   However, the end of the roller usually has a slight bevel, and
even in the positions shown in Fig. 3–16(b) and (c), the paint would not
cover the edge of the junction.   To reach these inaccessible areas,
special corner rollers, illustrated in Fig. 3–17, have been designed.
These are usually made of polyurethane or sponge rubber foam.

3.6 HOW TO SELECT A ROLLER

It is possible to paint using only brushes, as professionals have been
doing for years, but a roller does simplify painting large areas.   If you
decide on a roller, *don't look for bargains.*   A cheap roller is a poor

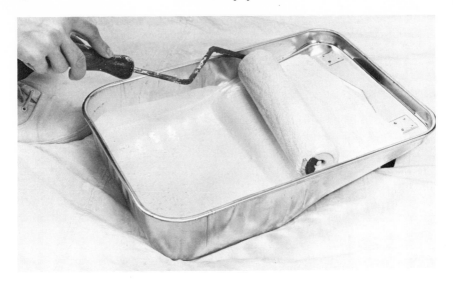

FIGURE 3–15. Roller and Pan. Photo Courtesy of PPG Industries.

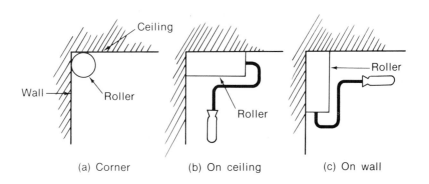

(a) Corner   (b) On ceiling   (c) On wall

FIGURE 3–16. Roller Positions.

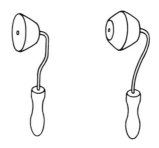

FIGURE 3–17. Corner Rollers.

investment unless you are planning only one paint job and intend to throw the roller away when you have finished.

Choose a good synthetic cover because you will use the roller with latex paint. Avoid cheap rayon covers. The nap should be ¼-inch high for most indoor painting, but if you are going to paint over plaster, gypsum board, or wallpaper, also get a cover with a ⅜-inch nap. Make sure both covers have a core that will not deteriorate when the covers are washed in warm water. The covers should be 9 inches wide.

The frame should be made of aluminum or stainless steel and should have a plastic handle. Again, the primary consideration is ability to withstand corrosion in water.

You should be able to slide either cover on the frame quickly and firmly, and once attached, the cover should rotate easily. If you don't like standing on a chair or ladder to reach the ceiling and upper parts of the walls, you should get a frame with a detachable extension handle.

The type of pan you use is not critical, but they are usually made of aluminum. This metal is lightweight, inexpensive, and does not rust when washed in water. For indoor painting, you will not need clamps that attach the pan to a ladder.

The small corner rollers shown in Fig. 3–17 are a convenience if you don't have any brushes. However, a corner roller is not easier than a brush to use and clean, and thus should not be purchased as long as you have a trim brush available.

3.7 HOW TO USE A ROLLER

A new roller should be conditioned before use. Wash the cover in soap and water to remove all dirt. After rinsing, you can use the roller immediately with latex paint as the roller can be wet when applying water-base paints. For alkyd paints, let the cover dry thoroughly before using the roller.

Paints that dry too quickly cannot be applied with a roller. This eliminates lacquers and fast-drying enamels, but most other paints can be rolled on. If you have any doubt, read the label on the can. In addition to telling you whether the paint can be rolled, the label will also supply special instructions for rolling. Many paints can be rolled as they come from the can, but some need to be thinned. The type and required amount of thinner is always specified on the label.

After you have stirred the paint well, pour enough in the roller pan to cover about half of the sloping part of the bottom. Every time you have to refill the pan, you should stir the paint before pouring it. Varnish, however, should never be stirred. Roll the paint roller in the paint in the deep part of the pan until the roller is filled evenly. Roll the roller on the exposed slope, as shown in Fig. 3–15, to remove excess paint. Now roll the paint on the wall, ceiling, or other flat surface. Apply the paint first in three or four strokes in a random pattern as shown in Fig. 3–18. This averts the roller's undesirable tendency to unload all the paint in one spot. Alternatively, you may make a large W on the wall with the first four strokes. Then, roll the roller across the first strokes, spreading the paint uniformly on the surface. Repeat this process, making your next random pattern or W a short distance away from the portion already finished. Blend in with horizontal strokes.

To avoid stooping and reaching, the pan should be placed about 2 or 3 feet above the floor. A small table or box covered with protective cloth or newspapers can be used. To reach a high ceiling, use an extension handle.

Do not press too hard as that causes the roller to paint unevenly. Roll it slowly and gently until the roller begins to get dry. Then dip it again and continue.

Cutting in is painting in the corners and other places that cannot be reached by a roller, such as around doors, windows, and baseboards. Cutting in could be done with a special corner roller, but it is simpler to use a brush, dipping it in the roller pan. Ideally, one person uses a brush, cutting in as shown in Fig. 3–19, while a second uses a roller on the flat surfaces. Cutting in should be done before the rolling, as the roller can blend the paint onto the cut-in section without brush marks. In Fig. 3–19, the ceiling is painted the same color as the walls. If a different color is used, some form of masking or careful trim painting is required. This is discussed in the section on painting specific parts of a room (see Chapter 5).

If you are interrupted while using a roller, simply drop the roller in a container of solvent (water, if latex paint is used). When ready to resume painting, roll the roller back and forth on some old newspapers until the solvent is almost dry and then continue painting as before.

3.8 HOW TO CLEAN A ROLLER

If you clean a roller as soon as you finish painting, it is a very simple task. The longer you delay, the more difficult it gets. Begin by rolling the roller on old newspapers to remove as much paint as possible. Pour some solvent in the tray for the paint you used. For latex paint, use warm water; for alkyds, use turpentine or mineral spirits. Rinse the roller cover in the solvent. When the paint is almost all gone, remove the roller cover from the frame and wash each separately in the

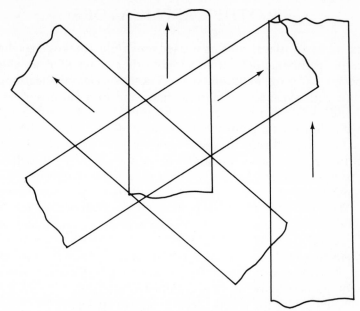

FIGURE 3–18. Random Roller Patterns.

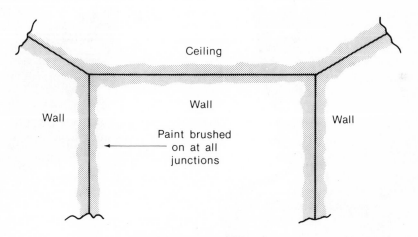

FIGURE 3–19. Cutting In.

solvent. For latex paint, you may find it simpler just to rinse the tools under a warm water faucet. For a final cleaning, no matter what solvent was used, rinse the roller in warm soapy water and then rinse out the soap. Hang it up to dry. Wrap the cover to keep off dust until the next job.

3.9 OTHER APPLICATORS

Since a napped surface, such as is used on a roller, makes a good paint applicator, paint manufacturers supply other convenient accessories for special painting requirements. These special applications are available with synthetic or natural naps and in a variety of shapes.

A handy tool for painting stairs is a *paint glider*, shown in Fig. 3-20. The pad is flat and is removable from the handle. The handle may be adjusted to any angle and locked there for ease in painting. The glider shown in Fig. 3-20 has a mohair pad and is about 6 by 3¾ inches, but larger pads are also available. For tight places and stairs where a roller is inconvenient, the glider is a useful addition to your set of painting tools. The nap side of a nylon fiber glider is shown in Fig. 3-21.

A glider may be used to paint a large wall; it is faster than a brush, but slower than a roller. In Fig. 3-22, paint is applied to a wall with a glider, starting with the same W pattern that is used with a roller. In general, however, you should use a roller for walls and reserve the glider for stairs, woodwork, and cramped quarters.

A special glider for sharp edges is shown in Fig. 3-23. A small

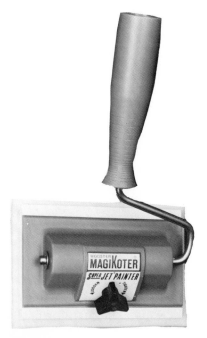

FIGURE 3-20. Paint Glider. Photo Courtesy of Wooster Brush Company.

FIGURE 3-21. Nap Side of Glider. Photo Courtesy of PPG Industries.

wheel or projection at the side is held in contact with a window frame, corner, or other surface that is not to be painted, and this keeps the pad itself away. Paint is deposited in a straight line with no danger of getting any paint on the clean surfaces. In the photograph, Fig. 3–23, the glider is being used to paint the inside stop of a double-hung window without getting paint on the sashes.

Another tool with a nap is a *painter's mitt.* This is simply a large mitten covered on the outside with a nap of wool or nylon. When the mitt is used, your hand becomes the painting tool. There is nothing better for painting pipes, posts, gutters, and many other round or irregularly shaped objects.

A roller pan is the best paint container to use with a glider or mitt. The same instructions on the can as to thinning that apply to a roller should be followed when using these applicators. Dip the nap into the paint, wipe off excess paint on the sloping bottom of the pan, and apply the paint to the surface much as you would with a roller. After the job is done, the glider or mitt should be cleaned immediately in the same manner as a roller is cleaned. (This is described in Section 3.8.)

For most indoor home painting, you need only a brush and a roller.

FIGURE 3–22. Glider on Wall. Photo
Courtesy of PPG Industries.

FIGURE 3–23. Edging Glider. Photo Courtesy of PPG Industries.

If you buy a mitt for painting pipes or a glider for stairs, you should choose a nylon nap since this is best for use with latex paint.

3.10 SPRAYING

Another way to apply paint is by spraying. For small jobs, paint can be purchased in a spray can for quick touch-ups or a complete paint job. There is no cleaning up afterward. For larger jobs, a spray gun is used. It is not necessary to buy a gun since most paint shops will let you borrow or rent one as needed when you buy the paint. Ask your paint dealer to set the controls for the paint and the job.

Paints that are sprayed must be thinner than those applied by brush or roller and should be thinned with appropriate solvents. Once the mixture is in the gun, spraying is very simple. You can spray almost any kind of paint on almost any surface, including cloth, leather, paper, metal, plastic, masonry, and wood. For wicker furniture and odd-shaped pieces, spraying is the fastest way to paint, but extra precautions are necessary. It is almost impossible to control the *overspray;* that is, spraying beyond the object being painted. Thus surrounding objects must be protected more thoroughly than when using a brush or roller. Adequate ventilation is necessary, and even outdoors you should wear a mask. For long jobs, you should also wear a cap and gloves.

Mix and strain the thinned paint before putting it in the gun. The spray gun or can must be moved so that the spray is perpendicular to the surface being painted and so that the nozzle remains at a constant distance from the surface, as shown in Fig. 3-24. In Fig. 3-24(a), the path of movement remains constant. This is correct. In Fig. 3-24(b), the gun is moved in an arc so that the distance between the gun and the surface varies; this will result in an uneven paint layer. If the surface to be painted is curved as, for example, the outside of a barrel, then the spray gun must follow a curved line to remain equidistant from the surface. This is shown in Fig. 3-25.

The tip of the nozzle should be about eight inches from the surface. This may vary with different spray guns and different aerosol cans, so make it a point to read the label first before using the equipment. Before you begin painting the surface, you should practice on a piece of cardboard or wood scrap. As you move the gun over the surface, the

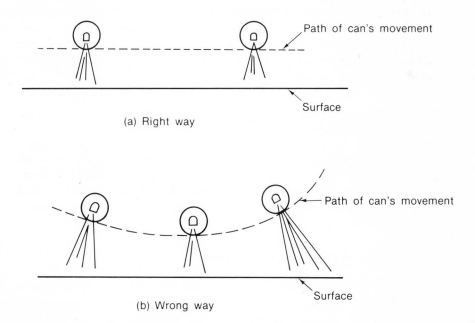

FIGURE 3-24. Movement of Spray.

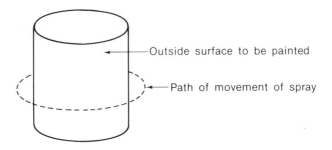

FIGURE 3–25. Spraying on Curved Surface.

gun should spray continuously. Do not start or stop the spray in the middle of a stroke. Start the spray with the gun pointing slightly off the surface. Then move the spray all the way across until the spray is off the surface at the other side. When coming back, always overlap your strokes. There will be no lap marks.

Always save the best for last. That is, when spraying furniture, start with the undersides of chairs and tables and other inconspicuous places. Finish on the best surface. The reason for this is that it is impossible to avoid some misting. If you did the top first, the misting from the rest of the job might cause the top to look sandy. Rubber-base paints exhibit less misting than others.

To clean the spray gun, empty the paint tank and wash it in the proper solvent for the paint you used. Then fill the tank with solvent and spray it through the gun until it comes out clear. Return the clean spray gun to your dealer.

3.11 OTHER ACCESSORIES

Before you begin painting, check off the accessories you may need and make sure you have them available. You may not need all of these items for every paint job, but it is better to have them on hand than to have to interrupt your painting while you hunt up a necessary tool. Here is the list:

Brushes

Roller and tray and other applicators

Paint buckets and stirrers

Stepladder

Dropcloths

Newspaper and clean rags

Putty or other fillers

Paint shield

Masking tape

Thinners

Sandpaper

Putty knife

Screwdriver

Hammer and nail set

Rubber gloves

Painter's hat

Some of these items are needed in preparing the surface, others in the actual painting, and some for cleaning up afterward.

You will most certainly need a stepladder or something to stand on to reach the junction of walls and ceiling. Even if you have an extension handle on your roller, you will still have to cut in with a brush. You can stand on a solid chair or table, but do not risk standing on a box on top of a chair. A convenient platform can be made from a plank and two chairs and will enable you to paint a large part of the ceiling with a minimum of climbing up and down.

No matter how careful you are, you will drip paint. You will need some sort of protective covering for furniture and floors. Dropcloths are available made of canvas, cloth, or plastic. In a pinch you can use old newspapers. When you have covered the areas to be protected, you don't have to worry about dripping and thus can paint more freely and with greater speed.

For painting close to a surface that is not to be painted, you need masking tape or a paint shield. Inexpensive metal or plastic shields are available, but you can get by with a piece of ordinary cardboard. Use of a cardboard shield to keep paint off the window glass when painting a sash is illustrated in Fig. 3–26.

You need some common tools: (1) a hammer and nail set for driving nails below the surface; (2) a putty knife to spread putty or filler in cracks and over nailheads so that the surface is smooth and unbroken; and (3) a screwdriver for removing hardware that is not to be painted. You will need containers for mixing paint and for holding solvents when you clean your painting tools: you can use old coffee cans or old paint cans. If you want to save old paint cans for this purpose, clean them with the appropriate solvent as soon as you have used up the paint. Cans from latex paint can be washed in water. Old paint cans are especially handy for holding paint because they have handles. If you want to avoid a large part of the cleaning process, buy

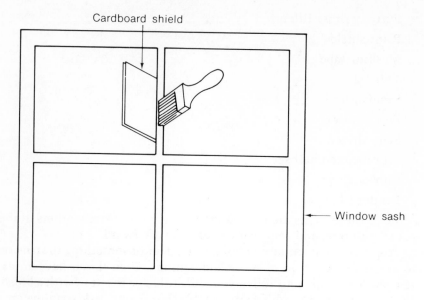

Cardboard shield

Window sash

FIGURE 3–26. Paint Shield.

inexpensive cardboard paint buckets and throw them away when the job is finished.

Even if you have dropcloths, you should have some old newspapers to wipe rollers and brushes. A good supply of torn sheets and other clean rags enables you to wipe up a mistake, such as painting on glass, easily before the paint hardens. Rags are also useful for wiping your hands and face. To protect your hair, it's best to wear a painter's cap, and to protect your hands, if you handle irritating chemicals, wear plastic or rubber gloves.

4

Getting Ready

Paint is not permanent. Eventually a painted surface wears, shows flaws, or appears dingy and the homeowner decides to repaint. If care is taken in preparing the surface before painting, the time between paint jobs can be lengthened. Surface preparation is the most important aspect of a paint job. A properly prepared surface will hold its paint without flaws three or four times as long as paint applied with little or careless preparation.

In addition to preparing the surface, getting ready implies having everything available so that work can proceed without interruptions. It also means arranging protective coverings, moving furniture, and anticipating all the small chores that must be done when painting.

4.1 GRIME AND GREASE

In a typical situation, you look at your walls one day, the paint looks dingy or worn, and you decide to repaint. The ceiling looks fine, so you will limit your repainting to the walls. After the walls are refinished, the ceiling looks dingy in comparison, and now you drag out all your equipment again to repaint the ceiling. You might have anticipated this and repainted walls *and* ceiling, regardless of relative dinginess. However, unless the paint was cracked or worn from repeated washing, the paint job was probably unnecessary. You can frequently restore a dirty or greasy surface to a bright finish simply by washing it. Soap and warm water will take off the dirt. For stubborn stains and grease, use a detergent. Rinse and wipe with a sponge and clear water. Mildew is unlikely indoors, but sometimes does occur on kitchen or bathroom walls where there is excessive moisture. Mildew looks like dirt, but cannot be washed off with soap or detergent. It does, however, yield to ordinary household bleach.

If you do decide to paint because, for example, the paint is worn thin after much scouring or because you're just tired of the color and want a new one, dirt and grease are still apt to be problems. Paint will not adhere well to grease, and over the years, some grease on walls and ceilings is unavoidable. This is especially true in kitchens where cooking vapors contain droplets of grease that are deposited on everything, but oils from finger marks can occur in any room in the house. Before painting any surface, check for grease by running a finger over it; if the surface feels too oily or waxy, wash off the grease with warm water and trisodium phosphate (TSP) or any household detergent. Wash off the detergent with clear water and wipe dry with a sponge.

If the wall is not greasy but does have dirt marks or stains on it, washing is usually unnecessary because the paint will cover the dirt. One exception is a greasy stain. The grease must be washed off although it is not necessary to remove all traces of the stain.

Loose dirt or dust in a room can be a problem since painting can stir it up, and then the dust will settle on the wet paint, spoiling the finish. If the walls and other areas to be painted are in good condition, dusting and vacuuming may be sufficient surface preparation. Don't forget to dust the tops of doors and window ledges. Dust anywhere in the room can spoil a paint job.

4.2 NAILS, HOLES, AND CRACKS

Preparing the surface involves sealing holes and cracks and covering nails so that their heads do not show through the paint. Before cleaning the surfaces to be painted, check to see if any other work is necessary and save the cleaning for the last step before painting.

In extremes of heat and cold, your house expands and contracts, and as a result, nails are apt to be pulled loose so that nailheads become visible. This occurs most often on walls of gypsum board. If the nails are simply driven back in the same holes, they will not hold as firmly because the original nail holes will have been worn. On walls where nailheads have become visible, the nails should be driven back in, but in addition, a few extra nails should be added between those already in place in order to strengthen the bond. The nailheads should be driven into the gypsum board so that the hammer dents, but does not break, the paper covering. The nailhead will then be below the surface of the wall. Fill the dent with spackling compound and, when it dries, sand it smooth with the wall. When you clean, make sure you dust off the loose spackling compound. Now you can paint over the surface, and the nailheads will not be visible.

Spackle or *spackling compound* is available as a white powder that is mixed with water to form a paste. Vinyl-base patching materials can also be purchased already mixed and ready to apply. The vinyl-base mixture is more expensive, but you don't have to worry about getting the proper ratio of water to powder. Latex paint can be used over either compound. For other paints, a primer is usually required.

When a floor squeaks, it is usually a sign that nails have become loose. Drive in a few flooring nails in the area where the squeaks occur. The nailheads should be driven below the surface with a nail set, and then the holes above the heads should be filled with putty or plastic wood. When the seal dries, you can paint over it, hiding the nailhead.

Cracks in plaster or gypsum board walls should be filled with spackle or ready-mixed sealer. Follow the directions on the can. Before applying spackle to a plaster wall, soak the wall around the crack with water, since the plaster tends to absorb moisture rapidly and if it were dry, it would draw the water out of the spackling compound too rapidly, causing it to crumble. This soaking is not necessary with ready-mixed sealers. For small cracks, simply apply the filler with a putty knife as shown in Fig. 4–1.

For larger cracks, you must make sure the filler is bonded to the plaster. Clean out the hole, removing all loose plaster, and cut the edges to form an inverted V all around the opening. Now when the filler is added and dries, the V holds the patch in place. Larger cracks may have to be filled in two stages. Put in some filler to about ⅛ inch below the surface. When this is dry, add enough to complete the job. This allows for shrinkage during drying.

For larger holes, such as might be present if you removed an electric fixture, first cut a plug of wallboard to the shape of the hole. This should be of such a thickness that when pressed against the studs or lathing, its surface is slightly below the surface of the wall. Attach the plug to the stud or lathing with a nail and patch on top of it to fill the hole.

After all cracks have been filled and patches sanded, you can clean the room. Loose dust from sanding and old plaster chips should be removed in the cleaning process.

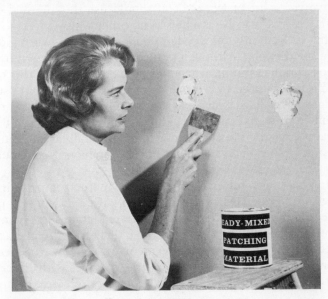

FIGURE 4–1. Patching Holes in Wall. Photo Courtesy of Wallcovering Industry Bureau.

4.3 HOW TO REMOVE OLD PAINT

For most paint jobs, you can paint over an old coat of paint, just making sure the surface is clean. You can even paint over high-gloss enamels, which normally provide a poor bond to a new coat of paint, by roughing up the surface slightly. The easiest way to do this is to wash the surface with a saturated solution of trisodium phosphate (TSP). This takes off the gloss and washes the wall at the same time.

You cannot paint over calcimine, whitewash, and similar water-base washes because paint won't stick to these coatings. However, you can remove any of these coatings with TSP or a detergent and warm water. Use a scrubbing brush dipped in the solution and scrub vigorously until the calcimine or other wash is removed.

If the old paint is cracked, flaking, or otherwise damaged, you must remove it before applying a new coat. There are many ways to remove old paint including scraping, sanding, sandblasting, application of heat, and chemical treatments. Your choice depends on the surface and the amount of time and effort you wish to put into the job. Cost may also be a factor.

Scraping is done with a tool called a *scraper*, which is simply a steel blade clamped to a wooden handle. In operation you pull the blade across the paint, pressing down hard as you do so. The blade gets dull quickly and must be sharpened frequently. You can also scrape with a putty knife or beer-can opener. Scraping is inexpensive, but it involves a lot of work. You should use this method only on small surfaces that can be reached in no other way.

Sanding is used only on wooden floors. Special power sanders can be rented for the job. Although you could conceivably remove paint from woodwork by sanding, it would be too tedious to use this method.

Sandblasting is used to remove paint from large masonry surfaces. It is almost never used indoors. You could rent equipment to sandblast paint from walls and floor in a basement, but it would be better just to paint over the old coat, since rental of sandblasting equipment is expensive. When such equipment is used indoors, you should use a mask.

Heating is an easy, relatively inexpensive method of removing paint from large surfaces. Heat may be applied with a blowtorch, propane torch, electric heater, or even with an infrared lamp. The paint is *not* burned off; it is simply heated until the old coat is softened and then is scraped off easily with any convenient tool. However, heating is dangerous because there is a danger of fire. Torches with direct flames can ignite the surface underneath or scorch it. Electric heaters may also cause a fire by overheating. Lamps are not too dangerous, but they are not very effective sources of heat.

To use a torch or electric heater, apply the heat without actual contact between flame or heater and the surface. When the paint begins to bubble, move the heat source with one hand while you scrape the soft film off with a putty knife held in the other. Some electric heaters have a built-in scraper so that in effect the heater and scraper are held in one hand.

Chemical paint removers are the most popular agents for removing paint. They are expensive and thus are not generally used for large walls. But then, in most cases, large walls are repainted over existing coatings without bothering about paint removal. **WARNING:** Chemical paint removers are poisonous and may be flammable. When you use them, you should wear gloves and protective glasses and make sure the room is adequately ventilated.

Chemical removers come in two forms, paste and liquid. Liquid removers are faster and can reach into crevices, but they cannot be used on vertical surfaces. Paste can be used on any surface, but is slower-acting than the liquid. Some removers have a water base. After using the remover, wash the surface with water to remove all traces of the chemicals. Wax is sometimes added to a remover to retard evaporation. After a remover containing wax is applied, all traces of the wax must be washed off with turpentine or similar solvent, and then the turpentine must be washed off with water if latex paint is to be used. The turpentine can remain if alkyd paint will be used.

Make sure you read the label before using the chemical and heed all warnings. You can apply the remover with an old brush or a rag. Let the remover soak in and soften the paint until you can wipe it off with a piece of rough cloth or steel wool. On walls, use a putty knife or spatula, but it must be cleaned frequently by wiping with old newspapers.

4.4 PREPARING PAPERED WALLS FOR PAINTING

You can paint with *latex paint* directly over wallpaper. Alkyd paints do not adhere well. The same general rules for preparation apply. The paper must be clean and well fastened to the wall. Never paint over dry-strippable paper since this type can be removed with ease.

If the wallpaper has greasy stains on it, wash it with water and soap or detergent. Modern papers are washable, and grease can be removed without too much difficulty. Loose dirt and dust must be removed. Wipe off excess water with a dry sponge.

If the paper is peeling or torn in several places, it should be removed before the wall is painted. Removing wallpaper is described in Section 8.5.

However, if there are only a few bubbles where the paper has pulled away from the wall and the paper is otherwise sound, it is not necessary to strip it. With a sharp knife, cut two slits in each bubble to form a cross. Lift up each of the four corners and apply some glue or paste to the back. Then press the paper back to the wall, wiping off any glue that squeezes through with a rag or sponge. When the glue dries, you can paint over the paper.

4.5 PREPARING WOOD

Wood floors require special treatment (which is discussed in Section 5.5), but there are many other wooden surfaces in a house. These include window trim, doors, woodwork, paneling, and furniture. The general rules for preparation apply: fill holes, sand smooth, and clean off dust and grease.

Holes, scratches, and dents can be filled with special wood fillers. If nailheads are visible or new nails are driven in, drive the heads below the surface with a nail set and fill the holes. Some fillers can be applied directly; with others, the wood must be primed first. Always read the instructions on the package. After the filler is dry, the surface should be sanded smooth and then wiped clean.

Knots in wood are a special problem. If they are loose, glue them in place and then sand the surface smooth. Because knots may exude resin that could bleed through the paint job, they should be sealed with a knot sealer or ordinary shellac. Sand the shellac lightly so that the paint will adhere to it better.

Defects should be removed. If there are burned areas, sand down to bare wood. If a part of a board is broken, cut out the broken piece and replace it with a new piece cut to shape. Make sure nailheads are set below the surface and covered with filler. If the wooden surface has an old paint coating that is peeling, strip off the paint as explained in Section 4.3.

4.6 PREPARING METAL

Metals may require careful surface preparation to make sure that the paint adheres well. The preparation depends to some extent on the type of metal and whether it has been painted before.

Ferrous metals, iron and steel, rust easily when exposed to dampness. If there is any trace of rust on the surface to be painted, remove it with steel wool or a file. Then clean with a suitable solvent. As soon as the metal is clean, apply a metal primer that inhibits rust. If bare steel is left exposed for even a short time, moisture in the air can cause it to rust again. For the same reason, water should not be used to clean the metal. Thus, mineral spirits, naphtha, or similar solvents must be used. Water-base paints should not be used on ferrous metals, but a latex metal primer is available for use under latex paint.

Aluminum also oxidizes in the air, but unlike rust, the oxide is hard and takes paint readily. Aluminum must be clean before painting. New aluminum usually has an oily film that can be washed off with warm water and soap or a solvent. Brass and bronze also tarnish in air, and like aluminum, paint adheres well to their oxides also. If any of these metals has old lacquer on it, the lacquer should be removed before new lacquer or paint is applied. Use lacquer thinner to remove the lacquer and wash it off with undiluted household ammonia.

If the metal surface is covered with an old paint film that is in good condition, you can paint over it. Just make sure the old paint is clean. Wash off dirt and grease with TSP or detergent and warm water.

4.7 PREPARING MASONRY

Masonry in the house, such as a fireplace or basement walls or floor, does not need paint for protection. However, you may decide to paint this type of surface for ornamentation or for ease in maintenance. Since latex masonry paint can be applied directly to masonry, you need only make certain that the surface is clean.

If a brick fireplace has loose mortar, scrape the loose particles free before painting. Then put in new mortar. Wash the surface and sweep up all dust before painting.

If masonry has an old paint finish on it, you can generally paint over it as long as the finish is in good condition. Rarely will you have to remove paint from a masonry surface. If there is some peeling, loosen as much of the old paint as possible with a wire brush and then feather the edges of the remaining paint.

4.8 ELECTRIC FIXTURES AND HARDWARE

Before you begin to paint a room, you will have to decide whether to paint over hardware and lighting fixtures or leave them unpainted.

Usually, switch plates and outlet plates are painted the same color as the walls, but doorknobs and lighting fixtures are not painted.

Whether or not you are going to paint switchplates and outlet covers, you should remove them before painting, as shown in Fig. 4–2. If you leave them on the wall and paint over them, some paint may seep behind them. When this dries, it will be impossible to remove the plates without damaging the surface. If you want to paint the plates, spread them on a pile of old newspapers and paint them when you paint the wall. To make sure you will remember to paint the heads of the screws and, incidentally, to remember where the screws are, put the screws back in their holes with the plates removed. When you paint the wall, you can touch the heads in passing.

Light fixtures are rarely moved, but, again, if you try to paint close, some paint can seep in and stick the fixture tightly to the wall or ceiling. Then, if you have to get at the electric circuit underneath, you may damage the wall. To avoid this, unscrew the fixture and let it hang by its wires. When the paint is dry, you can fasten the fixture in place again.

Similarly, it is easier to paint doors if doorknobs, strikerplates, hinges, and locks are removed first. With hardware removed, you can paint rapidly and more than make up the time and effort required to

FIGURE 4–2. Removing Electrical Switch Plate. Photo Courtesy of Wallcovering Industry Bureau.

take off the parts and put them back. In Fig. 4–3, a roller is used to paint a door with the doorknob removed. No cutting in around the knob is necessary.

Before you begin painting a room, you will, of course, take down curtains, draperies, and all pictures on the walls. If the pictures are to be put back on the same hooks, no other preparation concerning them is required. You can paint the hooks the same color as the wall. If the pictures will be moved, pull the hooks and seal the holes before painting. The hooks can be put in their new positions before or after the walls are painted.

4.9 PROTECTING FLOORS, FURNITURE, AND OTHER SURFACES

The first step in getting ready to paint a room is to clear everything out of the room. The time spent moving everything out and back is small compared to the time you will save by not having to climb over and around furniture. Unfortunately, it is not always possible to move everything out, and some compromise may be necessary. If you are going to paint only the walls, leaving the ceiling untouched, you can

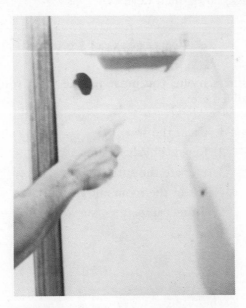

FIGURE 4–3. Knob Removed from Door. Photo Courtesy of Pittsburgh Paints— Products of PPG Industries.

move all furniture into the middle of the room, leaving a passageway next to each wall. If you are going to paint the ceiling, move the furniture to one end of the room and paint the ceiling at the other end. Reverse ends and do the other half of the ceiling. Finally, move the furniture to the middle and paint the walls.

If the furniture remains in the room, it must be protected by covering it with dropcloths. Flat surfaces such as tables can be covered with newspapers. The floor must also be protected, whether the furniture remains in the room or is taken out. Again, dropcloths or newspapers can be used.

When painting a wall close to the floor, you should use a paint shield to keep paint off the floor. Nevertheless, don't depend on the shield alone to protect the floor. Spread newspapers to cover the floor up to the walls.

If you wish, you can use a paint shield in many tight places, such as on door panels, on window sashes, and at junctions where two different color paints meet. If you want to avoid using a shield, before painting, stick masking tape on the surfaces to be protected. After you finish painting, you can pull off the tape and the excess paint with it. Masking tape is available in widths of up to 4 inches. For most applications, if you are careful, you can use a 1-inch tape. If you want to be freer with your brush, buy 2-inch tape.

4.10 SUMMARY

Before you paint a room, you must get the room ready for painting. The steps involved are:

1. Clear the way
2. Repair physical damage
3. Prepare the surface to be painted
4. Clean the room and the surfaces
5. Protect unpainted surfaces

5

Painting

After you have prepared the surface and moved the furniture, as mentioned in Chapter 4, you are ready to begin painting. If you work conscientiously, you may expect to use somewhat less than a gallon of paint per person per day. A gallon of paint covers from 200 to 500 square feet, depending on the surface. Rough, porous surfaces require more paint. A second coat always requires less paint than a first coat. If you figure about 350 square feet per gallon and 350 square feet per day, you will have a rough estimate of how much paint you will need and how long the job will take. When you order paint, buy one or two extra cans and arrange with the paint dealer to allow you to return unopened cans for full credit. This ensures that you won't run out of paint in the middle of the job.

5.1 HOW TO HANDLE PAINTS

Paint is a mixture of pigment in a vehicle or carrier such as oil or water. The pigment is not dissolved in the vehicle, but is held in suspension. When a can of paint remains unused for an extended period of time, the pigment settles to the bottom of the can. Before the paint can be used, it must be mixed thoroughly so that the pigment is in suspension again. When paint is left in the can overnight, the pigment settles again, and the paint again must be mixed. If the paint is not mixed thoroughly, the color on the painted surface will vary. The pigment will be distributed unevenly so that its protective property will vary from place to place.

When you buy paint, the dealer will mix it for you on a machine if you intend to use it in a few days. The mechanical shaker agitates the can so that the pigment and vehicle are thoroughly mixed. Alkyd and oil paints can be used immediately after shaking; latex paints should stand unopened for about an hour before using. Never shake or stir varnish.

If you must mix paint yourself because you want to finish a partially used can, for example, you can ensure a thorough blending by following these steps. When you open the paint can, you will note that the oil has risen to the top. Pour off the surface oil into a clean, empty container such as another paint can or a cardboard mixing pail. Stir the remaining oil and pigment with a wooden paddle until they are thoroughly blended. Gradually pour oil back into the mixed paint, stirring as you do so. Finally, pour the mixed paint back and forth between the two pails several times.

Try to have enough mixed paint available to do the complete job, or at least a whole wall. Different cans of paint, even from the same batch number, may have slight differences in color. If you change cans when you go from one wall to another, the color change will not be noticeable; but if you change in the middle of a wall, it will.

If you add a thinner, as is usually required when you use a roller, make sure the thinner is right for the paint. Read the label. Do not add too much thinner. Here again, the thinner causes a slight change in color, and you must add exactly the same amount of thinner to each can of paint. Thinner is added in the same way paint is mixed. Add a little at a time, stirring constantly. Finally, pour the mixture back and forth between two containers.

The paint can tends to get messy as you work. The groove that holds the lid usually gets filled with paint, and the outside of the can is frequently wet with paint. As you put the lid back on the can when you are finished, the paint in the groove can splash out and make a mess. One way of avoiding this is to punch holes in the bottom of the groove with a hammer and nail. Most of the paint in the groove will flow through the holes back into the can. The lid seals the holes when it is in place. To replace the lid, put it over the groove and cover the whole can with a cloth. Then tap on the lid with a hammer. Any paint that splatters will soil the cloth, but nothing else. Another way to avoid the mess is to crimp aluminum foil all around the top edge of the paint can. When you are through, discard the aluminum, and the paint mess will go with it, leaving the groove free of paint.

Old paint is usually lumpy and should be strained before it is used. Cheesecloth or an old nylon stocking can be used as a strainer. Place the cloth over a clean container and pour the paint through it. Discard the cloth and the lumps.

When a paint job is to be continued the next day, the paint must be poured back into the can and the can sealed. Be careful about splashing paint when sealing. When the can is reopened, note whether a film has formed on the paint. If so, remove and discard the film before stirring the paint. You should clean out the brushes and leave them in thinner overnight.

When you are painting, you can use newspaper under the can to catch drippings. A better method is to glue a paper plate to the bottom of the can so that this drip catcher will move with the can.

When a job is completed, the equipment must be cleaned. If you used latex paint, simply wash everything in soap and water. Shake out all water from brushes or rollers and wrap them in newspaper to keep them free of dust. If you use turpentine or other thinners to clean your tools, pour the thinner into a shallow pan and put your tools in the pan also. Work the thinner into every part of the brush until all traces of pigment disappear. Then wash your tools in soap and water to remove the thinner, comb out the brushes, and wrap them in newspaper.

Save the dirty thinner. Pour it into a jar or coffee can that can be sealed with a plastic cover. After a few days, the paint will settle, leaving clear thinner that can be poured off and used over again. Store the clean thinner in a suitably labeled container. If it is flammable, make sure you indicate that on the label.

5.2 HOW TO PAINT A ROOM

Painting the walls and ceiling of a room is done from top to bottom. Paint the ceiling first, then the walls. Doors, windows, and woodwork are painted after the main areas of the wall are finished. Do baseboards last since your shoes might rub against them while you are painting the wall. It is assumed that all surfaces are in good shape and have been prepared as described in Chapter 4. Before you begin painting, stir the paint, even if it was stirred by the paint dealer when you bought it.

Paint the ceiling with a roller or a brush. You will find the roller easier and faster, especially if it is equipped with an extension handle. Paint in strips across the shorter dimension of the ceiling; you can paint each overlapping strip before the last edge dries. Latex paint is very good as far as hiding lap marks, but occasionally lap marks show up later if one strip is dry before the next is applied. Cut in at the corners and junctions of ceiling and walls with a brush or corner applicator. Also, cut in around baseboards, windows, doors, and other areas that cannot be reached with a roller.

Paint the walls with a brush or a roller, just as you did the ceiling. The best way is to have two people working together, one using a roller while the other cuts in the corners with a brush. This is shown in Fig. 5-1. Note the newspapers covering the floor right up to the walls. When painting a wall with either a brush or roller, a right-handed person should paint from right to left and a left-handed person from left to right. In this way, if you accidently touch the wall with your idle hand, you will be touching a section that has not yet been painted. You can also lean on or brace yourself against the wall without any risk of marring the paint.

After you have painted the room, look carefully for any spots you may have missed. Go over them with the same tool you used before. If you used a roller, touch up the spot with light, slow strokes of your roller. If you were brushing, cover the missed spots with the tip of your brush.

FIGURE 5–1. Teamwork Painting Wall. Photo Courtesy of Pittsburgh Paints—Products of PPG Industries.

5.3 HOW TO PAINT DOORS AND WINDOWS

When you paint a door or a window, you must remember to paint every part, and paint in such a way that wet paint on one part does not interfere with your painting another. Painting a window requires care; in order not to have to lean over painted surfaces, it is preferable to paint the window frame after the window is finished. Doors do not present quite the same problem, and you can paint the door frame before or after you paint the door.

If a door presents one unbroken surface, there is not much problem on deciding the order of painting. Remove doorknobs and other hardware. Paint the edges first with a brush. For interior doors, you can omit the bottom edge, since no one sees it, but for doors to the outside, the bottom edge should be painted to protect the door from moisture seeping under it. Remove the door from its hinges and paint the bottom edge with any quick-drying coating. Then rehang the door and paint the other edges. Finally, paint the surface of the door with a roller or brush.

If a door has panels, there is a preferred order of painting the parts to minimize the possibility of lap marks. This order is indicated in Fig. 5–2. First paint the edges, second, the moldings around each panel.

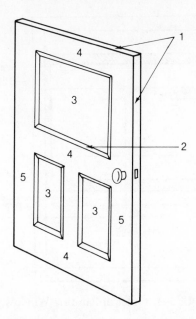

FIGURE 5–2. Order of Painting Door.

(Both of these are painted with a brush, but the rest can be done with brush or roller.) Third, paint the panels; fourth, the horizontal members, or *rails*; and fifth, the vertical members, or *stiles*. After painting, leave the door ajar until the paint has dried. Then replace the door-knobs and other hardware.

The order in which you should paint the parts of a double-hung window is indicated in Fig. 5–3. All parts are painted with a brush. First, raise the lower sash as high as it will go and lower the upper sash part way. Then begin by painting the checkrail on the top sash. This is the bottom horizontal member. Second, paint the horizontal and vertical bars that divide the sash into small panes. Some windows have such bars in one or both sashes, while others may have one large pane in each sash—in which case, this step is omitted. The vertical members (stiles) of the sashes are painted next. Throughout the fore-going procedures, it is necessary to raise and lower the sashes to get at the surfaces. You can grasp the horizontal rails of the sashes to do this since they are painted last.

When painting a window, you have to be careful to keep the paint off the glass. You can mask the window panes before painting or use a shield, as shown in Fig. 3–26, in Chapter 3. Alternatively, you can just try to be careful. Don't worry too much if you get a little paint on the glass. Let it dry, and then remove it with a razor blade. If a door has a

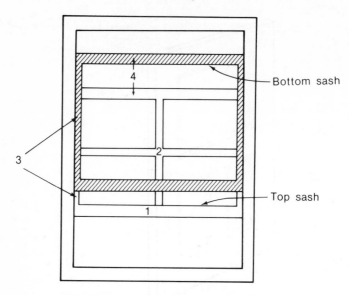

FIGURE 5–3. Order of Painting Window.

glass pane in it, paint the molding around the pane before painting the rest of the door. Use the same precautions to keep paint off the glass or scrape it off after it dries.

5.4 HOW TO PAINT A FLOOR

Interior floors are usually finished with a transparent coating, as described in Section 5.5, so that the natural grain of the wood shows through. Paint is opaque and hides the beauty of the wood. On the other hand, paint also hides any flaws and blemishes in the floor. Outdoor floors on decks and porches, for example, are usually painted, and some poor quality wood floors are also painted. Paint is sometimes used on concrete floors.

Any good quality paint will protect a floor, but specially designed floor paints will resist wear longer. The simplest to use is latex floor paint. You can apply this paint over a damp surface since it is water-soluble. It dries in about an hour. However, you should wait until the next day to apply the second coat. Two coats are usually sufficient, but on bare wood, a third coat is necessary. You can apply the paint with a roller or a wide brush.

Oil-base and alkyd floor enamels are the most common floor paints. They are more durable than latex paints. However, the cleaning up process is more involved. These paints cannot be put down on a damp surface.

Rubber-base paints are best for concrete floors, although the other floor paints are also quite satisfactory. Rubber-base paints should not be used on wood floors. Since gasoline attacks rubber-base paints, do not use these paints on a garage floor. Rubber-base paints cannot be applied with a roller because they dry too rapidly. Although these paints have excellent durability on concrete and masonry surfaces, the average homeowner should not use them because they are more difficult to apply, and special solvents are required for cleaning the equipment after the job.

Latex or alkyd floor paints can be applied with a roller or a brush. Latex paints are usually applied as they come from the can, but alkyd paint may be thinned with turpentine. Follow the instructions on the can. For concrete floors, a simple but effective method is to pour some paint directly on the floor and spread it with a stiff push broom.

5.5 HOW TO REFINISH WOOD FLOORS

When a floor has a few scratches in it, you can usually remove the damage without having to resort to a complete refinishing. If the scratches do not penetrate further than the finish, they can be removed with steel wool. If there are stains as well as scratches, use a cleaning agent with the steel wool. Rub only in the direction of the grain. When you have removed the scratched finish, smooth the surface with fine sandpaper or fine steel wool and apply a matching shellac or varnish. Dilute shellac slightly with alcohol; dilute varnish with turpentine.

If scratches are deep and penetrate the floor, remove the finish, as indicated above, and smooth the wood. Then fill the scratches with wood filler or wood plastic to a level above the surface of the floor. Remove the excess with a putty knife. When the filler is dry, sand flush with the floor using smooth sandpaper. Finish with shellac or varnish as above.

Refinishing a floor completely is not a difficult job, but it requires special equipment, which can usually be rented. There are three steps in refinishing: (1) sanding off the old finish; (2) applying a finishing coat of varnish or shellac; and (3) applying a coat of wax to protect the finish.

Before beginning the sanding operation, remove all furniture from the room, including pictures, drapes, and venetian blinds. Sanding leaves a thin layer of dust on everything. Look carefully over the entire floor, and if you see any nailheads, drive them down with a nail set. This is also a good time to nail down any loose boards or squeaky spots in the floor. Open the windows, shut the doors, and you are ready to begin.

You will need to rent a drum sander and a disc sander. The drum sander is used first to cover all large areas in the room. Sand parallel to the grain. Follow the directions supplied with the machine, and you will find it amazingly simple to operate. The disc sander is for edges that are not accessible with the larger drum sander. With both sanders, begin with a coarse paper to remove the finish and then progress to finer sandpaper with a second and third operation. Return the sanders.

After you have completed the sanding and before you begin the finishing, go over the *whole room* with a vacuum cleaner, including tops of doors, windows, and baseboards. Any dust left in the room can spoil the finish.

Finishes for floors fall into three categories. *Floor sealers* soak down into the wood and do not form a film or coating on the surface. *Varnishes, shellacs,* and some *synthetic finishes* form a surface coating that may be colored, but is usually transparent so that the grain of the wood is visible. *Floor paints* cover the floor with an opaque coating. The choice depends on the type of finish desired. Sealers and transparent finishes are covered in this section; painting a floor is discussed in Section 5.4.

If you want a matte finish on the floor, you should use a floor sealer. Apply the first coat with a brush or mop, or wipe it on with a cloth. If you wish to add color to the floor you can get colored sealer. Let the sealer remain on the floor for about 15 or 20 minutes and then wipe off the excess. After letting the floor dry overnight, rent an electric buffer and go over the floor. Now add a second coat of sealer in the same way. The sealer finish is usually scratch-proof. Worn areas can be touched up simply by wiping on more sealer, and there will be no danger of lap marks showing.

Varnish makes a pleasing finish, but it is slow-drying and therefore awkward to use. So-called "quick-drying" varnishes should not be used because they are not durable. Varnish can be put down over an old finish if the old finish is in good condition. For new or resanded wood, use a sealer for the first coat. After it has dried overnight, apply the varnish. You should put on at least two coats of varnish, waiting at least 24 hours for each coat to dry. Alternatively, you can use a coat of thinned shellac as a sealer and then two coats of varnish. Allow each coat to dry thoroughly before applying the next. A varnish finish darkens with age.

Shellac is simple to apply and dries quickly. White shellac does not stain the wood so that the natural grain is visible. Orange shellac also shows the grain, but darkens the wood somewhat. Shellac should be applied in thin coats. Shellac as purchased should be thinned with alcohol. Ask your paint dealer to advise you how much to thin it, since dealers may mix their own shellac already thinned. For bare wood, plan on putting on three coats of shellac, allowing each coat to dry at least two hours before putting on the next. Shellac is not as water-resistant as varnish, but it is easier to apply, and worn areas can be touched up easily.

Synthetic or plastic finishes are the most durable. They *require no wax* and will last for years. These finishes must be thinned with a special thinner and can then be brushed on easily. Two coats are sufficient. These materials are available in either a glossy or matte finish.

When your final finish is dry, you should wax the floor to protect the finish. Do not use a self-polishing liquid wax on a wood floor since these waxes contain too much water, which can damage wood. Paste waxes and solvent-based liquid waxes (not self-polishing) are satisfactory. Apply them with a soft cloth and let them dry about 20 or 30 minutes. Then use the electric buffer to polish. Two thin coats buffed separately give a longer-lasting shine than one thick coat.

5.6 HOW TO PAINT METAL

Metal surfaces, such as air registers or frames of casement windows, are no problem if they have once been painted. Simply clean the surface, as explained in Section 4.6, and, if the paint is not peeling, just paint over it with a brush as shown in Fig. 5–4.

If you are painting a wall with a roller, paint any air vent in the wall with a brush at the same time you use the brush to cut in the corners.

Latex paint can be applied directly to bare metals. However, since ferrous metals can rust when exposed to moisture, they should be primed before the latex paint is applied. Use special latex metal primers before painting with latex paint.

Alkyd and oil paints cannot be applied on bare metals without primers. Zinc chromate is a good primer, but be careful when using it because it is poisonous. Let it dry overnight and then apply the finishing coat.

5.7 HOW TO PAINT MASONRY

There are many different kinds of masonry paints, and they are not usually compatible. If you are going to use the same type of paint that

FIGURE 5-4. Brushing Paint on Metal Grill. Photo Courtesy of Pittsburgh Paints—Products of PPG Industries.

was used before, it is sufficient to clean the surface of dirt and loose paint and simply paint over it with the new paint. If the new paint is different from the old, or if you do not know what kind of paint was used originally, you will have to use a primer to make sure the new paint sticks.

Latex masonry paints are the easiest to use because they are thinned with water. Latex paint dries quickly and is very durable, but it cannot be used over old layers of alkyd or oil-base paint. However, there are latex primers available that adhere to the other paints and also make a good base for latex paint.

5.8 HOW TO FINISH FURNITURE

If you build furniture or buy ready-to-paint furniture, you can save money by finishing it yourself. "Finishing," when applied to furniture, means covering the object with paint, varnish, lacquer, or other film for protection of the surface as well as for the sake of appearance. A piece of ready-to-paint furniture is about 20 to 30 percent cheaper than the same piece finished. However, except for painting, finishing is a long, slow process. Although each coat may be put on quickly, the surface should be allowed to dry for at least 24 hours between coats, and at least four coats are usually required. In addition, the surface must be sanded or rubbed several times during the process. You must decide whether the saving you get by buying ready-to-paint pieces justifies the additional work.

If a piece of furniture is functional rather than decorative, such as for use in a kitchen or playroom, you may decide that it need only be painted. Paint covers the wood completely so that the grain is not seen. By the same token, paint covers blemishes and permits you to build furniture out of odd scraps of wood with grains or patterns that don't match. This would be impossible if you wanted a transparent finish such as varnish, shellac, or lacquer. The transparent finishes are used when the natural beauty of the wood should be visible through the finish.

Before beginning any finishing job, plan your work. Remove all hardware, such as locks, metal knobs, and handles before beginning. Drawers should be removed from chests or cabinets and stood on end with the front, the surface to be painted, in a horizontal position. Plan to coat the inside corners and hard-to-reach areas first. Save the easily accessible surfaces for last.

Painting is very simple. Any good enamel can be used. First, dust the surface thoroughly. Then, use a two-inch brush to apply an undercoat to the bare wood. This is usually a white enamel undercoat compatible with the final coat, but it can also be tinted. If you use latex enamel, the same enamel can be used for both undercoat and final coat. Only the two coats are necessary. The undercoat should be allowed to dry for at least 24 hours. Then the surface is sanded with fine sandpaper until it is smooth. Dust the surface thoroughly to remove all traces of dirt and grit. Then apply the final coat. After another 24 hours, the piece of furniture is ready for use. Paint should not be used on expensive, beautiful woods since it hides their natural beauty.

Varnish is tricky to apply. The biggest problem is air bubbles appearing on the surface, preventing a smooth finish. Therefore, you must never shake varnish and, if you stir it, do so very slowly. Dip the brush in the varnish so that only one-third of the length of the bristles is below the surface. Instead of wiping the excess off by drawing across the lip of the can, tap the brush against the edge of the can. This minimizes air bubbles. Pressing down too hard with the brush also causes air bubbles, so use a light pressure on the surface. Apply the varnish with long strokes. Special brushes for varnishing are available. These are very soft, with many flagged bristles to hold more varnish and fewer air bubbles.

The first coat of varnish may be thinned with one part turpentine to nine or ten parts varnish. Succeeding coats are not thinned. Each coat should dry at least 24 hours; after that the surface should be sanded smooth with very fine sandpaper. When sanding, always rub with the grain so that minute sanding marks do not show. Remove all dust before starting and after each sanding. Formerly, you had to rub the final coat by hand to produce a satin finish rather than what was considered an objectionable mirror-like surface. Now semi-gloss and flat varnishes are available for the final coat and need no rubbing. The glossy varnishes are tougher and are used for two or three coats first. Then a "satiny" varnish is used for the topcoat.

If you want something to protect the wood and are not too particular about appearance, apply one or two coats of shellac. Shellac may also be used on good wood since the grain shows through. For a fine finish on dark woods, apply about four coats of shellac, sanding each coat with very fine sandpaper. Shellac is not water-resistant.

Stain is used to color the wood without hiding the grain. It is easy to apply. However, on soft wood, stain soaks into the ends more than on flat surfaces, causing the ends to be darker. You can prevent this by first coating the ends with a thin layer of shellac. Stains can be brushed on easily since they do not show brush marks.

When the wood has been stained to the desired tone, you can protect the stain finish by covering it with clear lacquer. The only problem with applying lacquer is that it dries very quickly, so you must work as fast as possible without retracing your steps. Apply the lacquer in long strokes from one side of the surface to the other and have each stroke overlap the preceding stroke slightly. One problem is that the lacquer is clear so that you can't see whether you've missed a spot until it has dried. You can go back then and touch up these missed areas. You should apply at least three coats of lacquer; five is preferable. After each coat is dry (except the final coat), rub the surface smooth with a ball of very fine steel wool. Dust the surface before applying the next coat.

Refinishing furniture involves removing the old finish and then finishing by one of the methods described above. If you plan to use paint, however, it is not necessary to remove the old finish so long as it is hard. In fact, you may be able to get by with only one coat of enamel since the old finish can act as an undercoat.

You can remove the old finish easily with chemical removers. Buy one that is nontoxic and nonflammable. The general procedure is explained in Section 4.3, but always follow the instructions on the package. After removing the old finish, wash the wood with ordinary water to eliminate all traces of the chemical. When the wood is dry, you are ready for refinishing.

Before refinishing, make sure the surface is in good condition. If it is scratched, the scratches should be covered. If it has screw holes, knotholes, or cracks, fill them with a wood filler. The filler can be stained to match the wood. Light scratches can be removed by rubbing with furniture polish thinned with rubbing alcohol. Scratches in walnut can be stained by rubbing them with a piece of walnut meat. Scratches in mahogany can be touched up with iodine. Matching oil stains for most woods are available. After the surface is fixed up and dusted, finish as desired.

Kits are available for special finishes for furniture. Plastic and wood veneer laminates with adhesive backing can be applied directly to surfaces, even to surfaces built up out of scraps of wood. Antiquing kits enable you to make a new piece of furniture look like a genuine antique. Gold leaf and other special effects are all easily applied with kits on sale in building supply stores and mail order houses.

5.9 SAFETY

Before, during, and after painting, there are certain safety precautions that *must* be taken. The principal dangers are falls from ladders, chemical irritation, poisoning, and fire. At this point, you may think that the risks of harm outweigh the potential economic gain of doing the job yourself, but there is actually little danger so long as you are aware of the hazards and take simple precautions.

Exterior painting usually involves the use of ladders; indoors, similar problems arise when you paint a ceiling or upper wall. Use a stepladder rather than a box or a chair. A common practice is to place a board across two chairs or two ladders so that you can paint a larger area without having to go up and down too many times. This is safe as long as the board is solid enough and wide enough, *and you don't lean too far.*

Paint fumes may be toxic, especially if the paint contains lead or mercury. Fumes from solvents may also be toxic as well as inflammable. To minimize the dangers, always provide as much ventilation as possible when mixing paints, when painting, and when cleaning equipment afterward. When removing old paint with a scraper or blowtorch, paint dust may get into the air, and this can be very toxic if the paint contains lead. It is advisable to use a respirator when removing paint with a scraper or torch. This is not a danger when a chemical paint remover is used.

Paints and thinners can irritate the skin on contact. If you do get any solvent on your hands, remove it immediately. Better, wear plastic gloves when handling turpentine, naphtha or other solvents, or any chemical paint remover. Rubber gloves may also be used with most chemicals, but not with solvents for rubber-base paints. Plastic gloves are cheap and can be thrown away after each use.

Avoid the risk of fire by using nonflammable thinners and cleaners. If a flammable substance is used, dispose of rags in a tightly sealed metal container. Do not leave oily rags lying loose as they can ignite by spontaneous combustion.

When pouring paints or thinners, take care that there is no splashing that can irritate the skin or, worse, get in your eyes. It is not necessary to wear safety glasses when painting, but do take care not to touch your eyes or get anything in them.

Many of these precautions are unnecessary when you use water-soluble paints. You can also avoid the dangers of lead poisoning by using nontoxic paints. On children's toys and walls of children's rooms, *always* use lead-free paints.

II

Flexible Wallcoverings

6

Materials
and
Designs

Wall decorations date back to the time when man lived in caves. In medieval times, wallcoverings served a practical as well as a decorative purpose; they acted as insulation against cold and dampness. Woven material was usually used, and it was a small step to include a design in the material so that it would not be unsightly. In the homes of the wealthy, rich tapestries served both purposes. Wallpaper was originally conceived as an inexpensive decorative material for those who could not afford more expensive tapestries or patterned textiles. The wallcoverings that are pliable, like paper, are called *flexible,* as distinguished from *rigid* wallcoverings such as wallboard and paneling.

6.1 MATERIALS

Despite the fact that wallcoverings have been in use for centuries, technical advances are comparatively recent. Colors that did not fade were developed in the 1920s, washable colors in the 1930s. These two developments opened up new possibilities in design. Silk screen printing, in the 1940s, was a step in the direction of mass production. The 1950s saw the development of pre-pasted and pre-trimmed paper, making it easier for the home handyman to hang wallpaper without the aid of a professional. The most significant development in the 1960s was the widespread use of synthetic materials, both as a base and as a coating for paper cloth. Synthetic coatings led to the development of *strippable* wallpaper, which could be pulled off a wall without soaking or scraping. This was a boon to the handyman in that if he made an error in hanging, he could strip off the paper and put it back correctly. Also, when he got tired of the paper and wanted a new design, he could pull off the old strippable paper with little effort.

Vinyl is a synthetic material used in the manufacture of some wallcoverings. It is available as either a thin film or a liquid. In liquid form, it may be applied to a backing of paper or cloth to form a *vinyl-coated* covering. The term *vinyl wallcovering* is used to describe coverings of laminated vinyl and other materials. Vinyl may be laminated to paper, to cloth (either natural or synthetic), or to other synthetic bases. A laminate of paper and cloth that is coated with vinyl may also be referred to as *vinyl wallcovering.* Dry-strippable coverings usually contain vinyl.

Flocked wallcoverings feel like silk or velvet. To flock a wallcovering, the design is printed in varnish, shellac, or some similar sticky substance. Then, finely shredded fibers are spread over the covering, and they adhere to the varnish. The surface can then be coated to make the wallcovering washable.

Wallpaper designs are not printed right out to the edge of the roll, with the result that a white border remains on each edge. This border is called a *selvage*, and instructions for matching or hanging are sometimes printed there. The selvages also protect the edges of the papers from abuse during shipment and handling. The paperhanger has to trim off the selvage before hanging the material. Although it is possible to hang strips of wallcovering with edges overlapping so that only one selvage need be removed, the preferential method is a *butt* seam with no double thicknesses. Trimming selvages in a straight line to make an invisible butt seam is difficult, and to simplify work as much as possible for the home handyman, manufacturers offer *pre-trimmed wallcoverings*, with selvages removed at the factory. They are well worth the increased cost incurred by the added operation and extra care in handling the material.

Another improvement to make work easier for the handyman is *pre-pasted wallcovering*. Like postage stamps, the covering is backed with an adhesive that is activated when dipped in water. Instructions for hanging pre-pasted coverings are included with the materials, including the temperature of the water and the length of time to dip. To simplify the hanging procedure further, inexpensive water containers are available to be placed at the base of the wall being covered. For the handyman who prefers to apply paste himself, ready-mixed adhesive is available that is applied just as it comes from the can.

A *roll* or *bolt* of wallcovering is a standard unit containing 36 square feet, no matter how wide the strip. A double roll contains twice this, or 72 square feet. In practice, you should expect a roll to cover about 30 square feet since there is always some waste. A double roll will cover more than 60 square feet since waste is not doubled.

6.2 DESIGNS

There is no limit to the number of different designs that can be executed in wallcoverings. In fact, any imaginable design can be duplicated, and most have been, in existing wallcoverings. At one time, a design for a wallcovering fell into one of perhaps half a dozen categories, such as florals, geometrics, scenics, and the like. But it is no longer possible to limit even the categories since new ones are devised regularly.

Most wallcoverings are *patterned*; that is, the design is repeated regularly, usually on a single strip. The distance from the center of one element of a pattern to the center of the next is called a *repeat*. The distance is usually measured horizontally and vertically, and the two readings are called the *horizontal repeat* and the *vertical repeat* of the pattern.

Scenics or *murals* are wall decorations with pictorial designs that occupy two or more strips. A true mural does not repeat itself, but in wallcoverings, a mural may cover most of a wall and then be repeated around the room. The picture in a scenic wallcovering may be anything real or imagined. Pictures used include scenes from battles, historical incidents, mountains, lakes, rural scenes, statuary, nudes, and people alone or in groups.

Florals are probably the most common wallcovering patterns. Florals depict flowers, leaves, or plants, from realistic representations as they occur in nature to primitive imitations. *Geometrics* — designs that feature geometric shapes — are also popular. Geometrics include stripes, polka dots, plaids, checks, lattices, and the like. The difficulty of categorizing is evident when a covering has stripes or lattices with leaves or flowers twined around them. Is it a geometric or a floral? In any case, categorization is not important; the dealer who sells it probably calls it stripes and flowers. So too, geometrics themselves are better identified when they are called by what they show, such as a polka dot pattern, harlequin pattern, or whatever.

Wallcoverings can be made to imitate other materials, including designs used in cloth. Thus, there are damasks, paisleys, corduroys, and others that depict the design of the same name that appears in textiles. Also available are coverings that imitate wood paneling, basketweave, grasscloth, marble, and virtually any other material that one could conceivably want on a wall.

Wallcoverings can and do depict historic events in repetitive patterns and imitate the art of different periods. Thus, there are oriental motifs, renaissance designs, and even psychedelic, pop art, and op art designs. *Georgian* is in the style popular in England in the eighteenth century; *French Provincial* represents the rustic style of the French provinces in the same period. Other period designs include Louis XV, Louis XVI, Regency, and Jacobean.

Some designs copy designs used for other purposes. *Heraldic* coverings show motifs representing crests and coats of arms. *Tea-chest paper* designs depict the small geometric patterns used in the orient on paper in which tea is packaged. Bandbox designs show the kinds of motifs commonly used on bandboxes and hatboxes in the early part of the nineteenth century.

Ceiling papers are coverings with plain geometric patterns that can be viewed from any direction without looking as if they are upside down. Ceiling papers can be used to produce special effects. Thus, the strips can be cut in triangular shapes and hung so that the apices of the triangles are at the center of the ceiling. This is called *canopy ceiling* design. If the ceiling in a room is too high, it can be made to appear lower by bringing the ceiling paper down the walls to a border or molding. This is referred to as a *drop ceiling* design.

There are wallcovering designs for specific rooms in the home. Thus, *kitchen paper* may have a design featuring baskets of fruit or kitchen utensils. Nursery rhyme characters are usually represented on wallcoverings to be used in children's bedrooms. Coverings for a playroom or den may feature playing cards, monopoly layouts, dice, or other gaming devices.

One type of design that must be handled with extreme care is the *conversation piece.* This is the design that is so unusual or so cute that it is immediately noticed and draws attention from the rest of the room. Too often, a houseowner is struck by such a design and hangs the paper in a prominent place. It is indeed a conversation piece, but after "hearing" the same conversation day in and day out, one soon gets tired of it. When used with care in a room that is not used actively, such as a bedroom, conversation pieces can be very effective.

Manufacturers frequently put out *sets* of designs; that is, two or more designs that are compatible for use in adjoining rooms or on separate walls of the same room. For example, a simple rattan pattern may be used on one covering, and the same design with the addition of small flowers, twigs, or some other accent can be used on the second covering. The plain rattan design can be used on three walls of the room, and the accented design on the fourth wall. For use in adjoining rooms, designs should be different, but should not clash.

Most designs come in a variety of different colors so that you can usually find a design you like in a color to match the rest of your furnishings. For example, a simple floral may depict small white daisies on a solid color background. It would be available with a dark blue or dark green background for large rooms or with a pastel background for small ones. If you like a design, but the sample clashes with colors in your rug or furniture, ask to see the same design in other colors.

6.3 NAMES FOR WALLCOVERINGS

Manufacturers identify their designs by numbers, but since the buyer would have difficulty associating a number with a given design, they also name the design to make identification easier. The names sometimes reflect what is shown in the covering, but more frequently are chosen arbitrarily. Even when the name has nothing to do with the design, the buyer can associate the two. Thus, once a buyer sees a floral design called "Jane," he will recall the name if he liked the design, whereas he might have difficulty remembering #T–919.

Girls' names are used frequently to name designs, especially florals. "Clarissa," "Melissa," and "Jane" are florals. However, some florals are not given girls' names, and some girls' names are used for designs other than florals. "Suzanne" is not a floral. "Primavera," "First Love," "Bon Jour," and "Cheri" are all florals.

Some designs are given common descriptive names such as "Brick," "Lattice," "Denim," and "Gourmet." The last depicts foods and is a kitchen wallcovering. Many manufacturers use these same names, but where possible, they prefer names that are distinctive and hopefully will not be used by other makers. So names such as "Gourmet Delight," Kitchen Gourmet," and "Gourmet's Paradise" have replaced the simple "Gourmet."

Vertical stripes are a problem. Many manufacturers have several different striped patterns. Some are pin stripes, others wide; some are multicolored, others are monochromatic. The names reflect imagination. Rarely is a striped design referred to as a "Stripe." Names for stripes may be arbitrary such as "Cumberland," "Antoinette," and "Decorama." Some names do suggest thin, long objects, including "Pencils," "Candy Stick," and "Lollipops." Sometimes a name is nonsensical like "Don't Let the Rain Come Down," which is also a striped design.

Geometric designs are also given names that suggest figures, but hopefully are different from the names used by other manufacturers. Thus, we have "On the Square," "Superstar," "Parquet," and "Amazin." The last is a design depicting a maze.

Many titles name or suggest objects in the design. For example, "With a Twist, Please" depicts olives, and "On Parade" shows toy soldiers. "Shell-fish" shows shells and fish, and "Toy Shelf" depicts nursery toys. A stretch of the imagination is sometimes necessary, as "Morning Sun" for a design of birds and flowers.

Finding names that are different is a difficult task considering the thousands of different designs. Some names are frivolous or are obvious puns. Thus, we have "Cat Got Your Tongue" (a geometric) "Knots to You" (depicting knots), and "Dear John" (showing bathroom fixtures).

7

Factors Affecting Choice

When you decide to paint a room, you have to choose a color, but beyond this you have few problems of choice. On the other hand, if you decide to use wallcoverings, you must choose colors or combinations of colors and then make a selection from an almost infinite number of designs. Indeed, the very great variety of designs may scare you into giving up the idea of using wallcoverings and make you settle on a paint job instead. However, with a little thought and planning, you can unravel the mysteries of designs and take advantage of the unlimited decorative possibilities of wallcoverings.

7.1 PAINT VERSUS WALLCOVERINGS

If every wall of every room were painted, your home would have the monotonous look of a hospital ward. On the other hand, if every wall were covered with a fancy design, the result might be too giddy for comfortable living. Before considering the question of paint or paper, you should decide whether a room should have designs or plain walls.

As a general rule, rooms in which you are active should have plain walls. Game rooms fall into this category since designs only distract players from their activities. Also, rooms that have natural decorations like bookshelves, a fireplace, or a picture window should have walls that do not compete for attention with the built-in decorations. Similarly, rooms in which you plan to hang wall decorations do not need added design on the walls.

Rooms in which you spend little time can have interesting designs on the walls. Thus, a bedroom can have conversation-piece wall designs that might otherwise be cloying if they were in a living room. Rooms in which you do routine or boring tasks can have designs to make your work more interesting. This applies, for example, to kitchens, bathrooms, and laundry rooms.

Note that *design versus plain* is not the same as *paper versus paint.* There are wallcoverings with very plain patterns that can be used wherever paint would be satisfactory. However, if a design is indicated or would be preferred for decorative purposes, then a wallcovering should be used. If a wall should be plain, your choice as to paint or paper will be affected by factors of cost, convenience, and your experience in painting or papering. Although you can buy very expensive wallcoverings with custom designs, it is generally cheaper to paper than to paint. Good quality vinyl coverings with plain patterns have a lower initial cost than a good paint job and will wear much longer than a coat of paint. Painting is somewhat easier than hanging wallcoverings, but the latter has no mysteries, and men and women who never papered walls before have found they can hang wallcoverings proficiently after merely reading instructions. Wallpapering tools are cheaper than painting tools, although most homeowners already own paintbrushes and rollers.

In summary, you can find a wall covering suitable for any wall in any room. You may elect to use paint where a plain pattern is indicated, but you should use wallcoverings wherever a design can make a room more interesting.

7.2 COLOR THEORY

White light is a mixture of all the colors of the rainbow. In fact, a rainbow occurs when sunlight is refracted through raindrops so that each component color is bent by a different amount. When white light falls on a colored surface, a red wall for example, the pigments in the coloring on the wall absorb all the colors but red. The red light is reflected back to your eyes and the wall looks red. If the same wall were illuminated with a pure blue or green light, the light would be absorbed since the pigments would absorb everything but red. Then, since nothing was reflected from the wall, it would look black. Black is the absence of color.

Pigments have three *primary colors:* red, yellow, and blue. All other colors, including white, gray, and brown can be formed by a proper blending of these three primary colors. The color wheel in Fig. 7-1 shows the relationships among the colors. The primary colors are indicated by capital letters. The other colors are called *secondary colors.* Each secondary color can be formed by mixing the two primary colors on each side of it. Thus, orange results when red and yellow are mixed; green, from a mixture of yellow and blue; and violet, from red and blue. Notice that the color relationships are continuous around the circle. White is a blend of equal parts of the three primary colors, while browns utilize the three primaries in unequal proportions.

Two adjacent colors on the color wheel may be blended to form a new color. These *tertiary* colors are usually referred to by the names of the colors forming the new blend. For example, red-orange is a combination of red and orange, and blue-green is a combination of blue and green. In designating the tertiary colors, the primary color is named first. Decorators may use other names for some colors, such as tangerine for red-orange or aquamarine for blue-green; but in choosing colors for color schemes (see next section), the source of the color

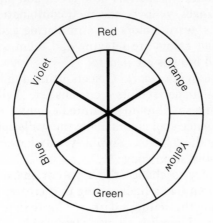

FIGURE 7-1. Color Wheel.

should be kept in mind. Tertiary colors are essentially the result of unequal mixtures of two primaries. Thus, red-orange is a blend of red and orange, but orange is a mixture of red and yellow. So red-orange is a blend of red and yellow, with red exceeding the yellow.

Opposite colors are called *complements* or *complementary colors*. Thus, red and green are complements, as are orange and blue, and yellow and violet. When complements are mixed together, the result is a shade of white or gray. This can be understood from the color wheel. Since green is a blend of yellow and blue, then a mixture of green and red is really a mixture of red, yellow, and blue, the three primary colors.

From a practical standpoint, no pigment is *monochromatic.* A monochromatic color is a pure color. Most colors that look like a primary color may in fact be a blend of all three primaries with more than 50 percent of the dominant color.

7.3 PROPERTIES OF COLORS

Colors affect mood; they can make a room seem larger or smaller, and can accentuate specific features of furnishings. In a sense, anything goes. If you like a particular color combination, there is no reason why you shouldn't have it. However, if you know what can be accomplished with color, you may be able to make a room more comfortable or more interesting instead of simply acceptable.

Colors may be classified as *warm* or *cool.* Greens, blues, violets, and their combinations, such as blue-green and blue-violet, are cool colors. Reds, oranges, yellows, and their combinations are warm. As the name implies, warm colors are stimulating and seem to advance toward you. Cool colors are relaxing and seem to recede. Whites, blacks, grays, and browns are *neutral.*

Colors may be *light* or *dark.* Objects painted in light colors appear larger, while those in dark colors seem smaller. Yellow makes objects appear largest. If a small room is painted a light, cool color, the room will seem larger since cool colors make the walls appear to recede and light colors make them larger. Similarly, a dark, warm color can make a large, empty room seem cozy.

The use of color to change the apparent shape of a room can be startling. If a room has a high ceiling that creates the impression of emptiness, making the ceiling a darker color than the walls will cause it to appear lower. Likewise, a low ceiling can be "raised" by painting it white and using darker colors on the walls. A square, uninteresting room can be made more interesting by covering one pair of opposite walls with darker colors than the other pair. The room will then appear rectangular. Alternatively, one wall can be made brighter than the other three, and it will act as a focus of attention.

A predominant color on the walls of a room will enhance the visibility of everything else in the room that is the same color. Thus, if you want to accentuate a rug, a piece of furniture, or a work of art, make a large area of the walls the same color as the predominant color in the featured object. A corollary to this is that too many different colors in a room make it featureless. Also, do not use different colors in equal proportion. One color should always be dominant.

Cool rooms can be "warmed" by warm colors. Rooms that face the sunny side of the house should be done in cool colors. Most rooms, however, should have both warm and cool colors. Don't use all neutral colors to avoid conflicts. Without some warm or cool colors, a room is too boring. However, some neutrals should be used to contrast with the other colors in the room.

There are four basic color schemes that are usually used to decorate rooms, but you should feel free to use your own imagination and plan a room to your liking. The four schemes, however, are a good starting point, and you should study them before letting your imagination roam.

1. A *monochromatic* scheme is built around one color. Walls, furniture, drapes, bedspreads are different shades or tints of the same color. This can be very effective in a bedroom, but may pall if viewed every day in a living room. If each bedroom

is done in a different color, the whole arrangement can be very harmonious.

2. An *analogous* or *related* color scheme is very popular and can be used in any room in the house. Two or three colors that are close to each other on the color wheel are the basis of the scheme, with accents furnished by small tinges of adjacent colors. Thus, green, yellow-green, and yellow may provide the predominant motif with accents of blues or oranges.

3. *Contrasting* or *complementary* color schemes are also popular. Here you must be careful. Red and green may look like perpetual Christmas decorations, but by combining unexpected tints of complementary colors, such as pink and dark green or pastel shades of both, you can soften the impact of the contrast.

4. An *accented* color scheme is a combination of the analogous and the contrasting schemes. The predominant areas are covered with adjacent colors, and the whole is boldly accented with a color from the opposite side of the color wheel.

7.4 DESIGN IDEAS

Like colors, designs can also change the apparent size and shape of a room. A low, cramped ceiling can be "raised" by using strong, vertical designs, such as stripes, on the walls. The maximum effect is obtained when the ceiling is lighter than the walls, as described in Section 7.3. To "lower" a high ceiling, call attention to it with a pattern on it; or run a ceiling paper down the wall to a border or molding. Use horizontal patterns on the walls.

Cool colors on the walls make a room seem larger. Combined with open patterns or scenics, the effect of spaciousness is enhanced. On the other hand, big patterns with plenty of bright colors can make a bare room seem well furnished.

A narrow room should have horizontal patterns on the short walls. The horizontal lines will make the other two walls seem further apart. Do not combine horizontal lines on one wall with verticals on the next as this is confusing. Use floral patterns on the long walls.

Design and colors go together to create an impression. The colors and design of a wallcovering must not only be harmonious with each other, but they must also blend with the furniture and decorations, especially with rugs, drapes, and upholstery. Further, designs in each room should be related to those in other rooms so that there is no "shock" of a sudden change of mood or impression.

The living room in Fig. 7-2 contains light-colored furniture and rug. A light-colored wallcovering might make the other colors look washed out, so a dark green covering was chosen to contrast with and bring out the warm yellows in the rest of the room. The upholstered chairs have a matching green accent, which is strengthened by the wall color. The small white bouquets on the wall break up the green expanse to give a more formal appearance than a solid color would have. The wallcovering is Thibaut's "Jane."

Another living room is shown in Fig. 7-3. This is a city living room, and the decorator wanted to create a mood of country intimacy in the city. She chose Academy's "Melissa" with large floral patterns in autumn colors to produce a feeling of warmth and snugness.

The living room in Fig. 7-4 has a geometric pattern in the sofa that is augmented by a different geometric pattern on the walls. The wall design, Thibaut's "Parquet," repeats the blues and greens in several of the upholstery fabrics, calling attention to the Chippendale furniture without making the room seem cluttered.

The wallcovering shown in Fig. 7-5 is Columbus Coated Fabrics' "Kitchen Magician," and is typical of many bright, cheerful kitchen designs showing food or kitchen utensils. In general, a kitchen or any work area should have light walls for an illusion of roominess and warm colors for a cheerful mood. It is not always necessary to choose

FIGURE 7-2. Formal Living Room. Photo Courtesy of Richard E. Thibaut, Inc.

FIGURE 7–3. Living Room with Floral Pattern. Photo Courtesy of Academy Handprints, Ltd.

FIGURE 7–4. Living Room with Geometric Pattern. Photo Courtesy of Richard E. Thibaut, Inc.

FIGURE 7–5. Kitchen. Photo Courtesy of
Columbus Coated Fabrics.

a design that says, "This is the kitchen." The most important requirement of a good kitchen wallcovering is that it be washable. The covering shown in the figure can be washed clean with a damp sponge and
will outlast a paint job.

The design of Fig. 7–6, Standard Coated's "Primavera," is a floral
that can be used anywhere. Here it is used in a bathroom on walls and
vanity doors; colors of towels and shower curtains are repeated in the
wallcovering. Like kitchen wallcoverings, those in bathrooms must
withstand moisture and be washable.

A geometric design was needed for the penthouse in Fig. 7–7 to
complement the contemporary setting of glass, steel, and plastics.
Schumacher's "Diamonds and Squares" is an intricate and intriguing
design lending a bit of interest and warmth to what could be a very
cold, functional room.

The two wallcovering designs in Fig. 7–8 show how striking patterns can dress up a room to create a feeling of luxury with inexpensive
furniture. An important aspect of covering the walls of a nursery or
a child's bedroom is to choose a design that will not seem too childish
as the children grow older. The coverings are "Superstar" and "Your
Father's Moustache," both by Columbus Coated Fabrics.

FIGURE 7–6. Bathroom. Photo Courtesy of Standard Coated Products, Inc.

FIGURE 7–7. Penthouse. Photo Courtesy of F. Schumacher and Co.

FIGURE 7–8. Boy's Room. Photo Courtesy of
Columbus Coated Fabrics.

A floral is always a good design for a dining room, as shown in Fig.
7–9. Here, the background color of Academy's "Mille Fleur" matches
and accents that of the chair seats. In dining rooms, the wall design
should not be so bold as to compete with the food for attention.

The wallcoverings in Fig. 7–10 illustrate how a good design can
"fill" an empty apartment. The jungle design, Thibaut's "Paradise."
in the dining room blends well with the colorful cloth covering a cheap,
secondhand table. The rattan design of Thibaut's "Rattan" in the far
room is related to the tropical motif of the dining room pattern and the
two present a unified decoration.

The "mood" of a room may be determined by the wallcovering and
should match the temperament or personality of the person who will
live there. The living rooms depicted in Figs. 7–2, 7–3, and 7–4 convey
different feelings of warmth, intimacy, or cool formality. Make sure
the design you choose is one you will be comfortable with.

FIGURE 7-9. Dining Room. Photo Courtesy of Academy Handprints, Ltd.

FIGURE 7-10. Apartment. Photo Courtesy of Richard E. Thibaut, Inc.

8

How to Hang Wallcoverings

Manufacturers of wallcoverings have added so many features for the handyman that hanging wallpaper is now a simple task. The instructions in this chapter cover the following steps in the process:

1. Measuring the room to determine how much to buy
2. Tools needed
3. Preparing the wall
4. Removing old paper
5. Hanging the wallcovering
6. Hanging pre-pasted wallcoverings

The procedure is not difficult, and most people who buy wallcoverings do their own hanging.

8.1 MEASURING

A *roll* of wallcovering contains 36 square feet of usable material, regardless of the width of the roll. When you buy a bolt of material, it may be a *single roll* or it may be a *double roll*, containing 72 square feet, or a *triple roll*, containing 108 square feet. When you hang wallcoverings and have to match the pattern from one strip to the next, there is always some waste. Taking waste into consideration, you should assume that a roll of material will cover about 30 square feet instead of 36. If the design is one that can be matched randomly, there will be very little waste. Also, there is less waste with wider rolls since fewer strips have to be matched.

Remember: You are covering the walls, not the floor. Therefore, you do not want the floor area. To find the area of the walls, first measure the distance around the perimeter of the room and multiply this by the height. Assume your room has the floor plan shown in Fig. 8-1. The perimeter is $14 + 16 + 8 + 5 + 6 + 21 = 70$ feet. If the walls are to be covered from floor to ceiling, then multiply 70 by the height of the room to get the area of the walls. In practice, there may be a baseboard and a molding, and the covering is to go between them. This is the height you must measure. Use a yardstick as shown in Fig. 8-2. Assume you find the height is 8 feet. Then the area of the walls is $70 \times 8 = 560$ square feet. Divide by 30 to get the number of rolls. When you divide 560 by 30, you get between 18 and 19. Then, the first approximation is that you will need 19 rolls. However, you are not going to cover doors and windows and you should subtract those areas. If you wish, you can measure everything exactly, but it is safe

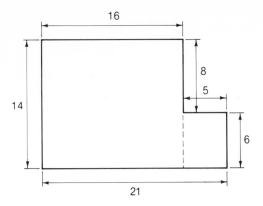

FIGURE 8-1. Room Dimensions.

FIGURE 8-2. Measuring Height of Wall. Photo
Courtesy of Wallcovering Industry Bureau.

to say that an average window or door is about half a roll in area. If
your room in Fig. 8-1 has four windows and two doors, you can simply
subtract 3 rolls from the 19 figured for the whole room. Thus, you
should buy 16 rolls.

If the wallcovering is plain, you may use almost all of it without
waste and cover almost 36 square feet with each roll. If your dealer
will permit it, arrange beforehand to return any unopened rolls for a

refund. Then you won't worry about whether you bought enough or too much for the job.

If you also intend to cover the ceiling, then you need to know the ceiling area. If the room is irregular, divide it into rectangles and add the areas of all the rectangles. The ceiling of Fig. 8–1, as indicated by the dotted line can be divided into one rectangle 14×16, or 224 square feet, and another 5×6, or 30 square feet. The ceiling area is then 254 square feet, and if you divide by 30, you see that it will take another nine rolls.

Borders are sold by the running yard rather than by area. If you plan a border on all or part of the wall, measure the length of the part to be covered by the border and simply give this dimension to your dealer.

A mural may be your choice for a large, unbroken wall. Measure that wall carefully and bring the dimensions to your dealer. You must match the strips or panels of a mural exactly, and you do not have the latitude you have with a repetitive pattern. It is well to make a sketch of the room with walls flat and plan exactly how the mural is to appear on the walls.

8.2 TOOLS

Tools for hanging wallcoverings are very simple and very cheap. You will need a paste brush, a smoothing brush, a seam roller, a plumb line, chalk, and a razor knife with extra blades. All of these items are included in a hanging tool set, obtainable at your wallpaper dealer. A typical kit is shown in Fig. 8–3. You will also need a paste bucket, a stepladder, a table, a screwdriver (to remove electric fixtures), a ruler, scissors, a bowl and sponge, and sandpaper. These are not included in the hanging kit since they are usually available around the house.

You may not need all the tools in the kit. For example, if you use a pre-pasted covering, you will not need a paste brush. However, the cost of the kit is less than the cost of all the tools bought separately, so you might as well buy the kit. If you use pre-pasted wallcovering, you will not need a paste bucket, but instead you will need a water tray, which is also very inexpensive. Unlike painting tools, bargain hanging tools will work just as well as expensive ones.

8.3 SELVAGES AND SEAMS

When wallpaper is printed, the design is not carried out to the edge of the bolt, but a small strip is left on each side. This strip is called a selvage (see Section 6.1), and it should be removed before the wall-

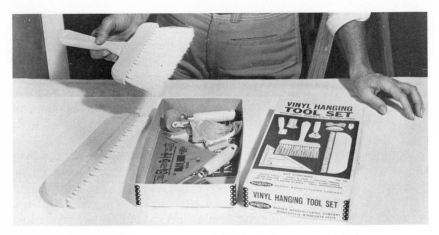

FIGURE 8–3. Hanging Kit. Photo Courtesy of Wall-covering Industry Bureau.

covering is hung. Most modern coverings have selvages removed at the factory and are called *pre-trimmed*. Some have perforations along the selvages. To remove the selvages, whack the tightly rolled bolt against the edge of a table, and the selvage will part at the perforations. Some delicate wallcoverings are neither pre-trimmed nor perforated. The selvages are left on these for added protection. However, you can buy pre-trimmed paper in most wallcoverings.

When you hang paper, the simplest way to make a *seam* is to butt one strip against the next without any overlap. This is called a *butt seam* and requires trimmed edges. It is the preferred method of making seams since there are then no double thicknesses of covering on the wall. If you are worried about butting strips exactly and fear an opening may allow the wall to show through, you can overlap the strips slightly, about 1/16 inch or less. This is called a *wire-edge seam*. The double thickness at the seam is only slightly noticeable. An *overlap seam* is used when only one selvage is removed. Each strip must cover the untrimmed selvage of the preceding strip.

8.4 PREPARING THE WALL

Before hanging a new wallcovering, you must remove any old paper. At one time, new wallpaper was simply placed over old, and it was not uncommon for a wall to have three to five layers of wallpaper. The dry-strippable coverings, however, should be placed on bare walls and not over other papers. If the old paper is strippable, pry off one corner and pull it from the wall. It should come off easily. How to remove old paper that is not strippable is described in the next section.

Remove all switchplates and outlet covers as shown in Fig. 8-4. Later, if you wish, you can cover the plates with a small piece of the same wallcovering material so that the switch will not be conspicuous. To do this, cut a piece somewhat larger than the plate, matching the pattern to that already on the wall, and paste it onto the plate with any kind of adhesive. Tuck the excess under and screw the plate back on the wall after cutting a hole for the switch button. Alternatively, you can replace the plate with an artistic plate that is compatible with the design of the wallcovering.

Before hanging the wallcoverings, make sure the wall is in good condition. Repair gouges and cracks in the wall. You can buy ready-mixed patching compound for this and apply it with a putty knife, as shown in Fig. 8-5. Sand down any rough spots. Finally, wipe or wash the walls to remove grease or dust.

8.5 HOW TO REMOVE OLD WALLPAPER

If the old wallpaper is not dry-strippable, it must be moistened and scraped off. You can use a mixture of warm water and vinegar or

FIGURE 8-4. Removing Switch-plate. Photo Courtesy of Wall-covering Industry Bureau.

FIGURE 8–5. Patching Wall. Photo Courtesy of Wall-covering Industry Bureau.

special wallpaper remover preparations that are mixed with warm water and apply the mixture with a sponge or mop to loosen the old paper. However, the fastest method is to use a wallpaper steamer, which can be rented from most dealers in wallcoverings. The rental cost is small compared to the cost of the wallcoverings.

A steaming machine has a boiler in which water is heated, by electricity in small units or by kerosene in larger ones. The steam from the boiling water is fed through a hose to a perforated plate that is held against the old wallpaper. The steam soaks into the paper, softening the paper and the paste holding it to the wall. The paper can then be stripped off the wall with a putty knife or any flat tool. A special tool for the purpose, called a *wall scraper*, looks like a very wide putty knife.

When using the machine, begin at the bottom of a wall since the hot steam tends to rise and will soften the paper above the plate as well as that directly under it. Move the plate upward slowly with one hand while you strip the paper below with the other. Make sure the room is well ventilated to prevent it from filling up with steam.

The steamer can also be used to remove wallpaper from a papered ceiling. However, if paper is to be removed only from walls and you desire to leave the old paper on a ceiling, you cannot use a steamer. The rising steam would loosen the ceiling paper. In this case, you will have to soak the paper on the wall by hand. When the paper is soaked, you will be able to strip it off with a flat tool.

After removing the old paper, wipe up all excess moisture as soon as possible. Patch the wall where necessary and clean and smooth it before hanging the new wallcovering.

8.6 CUTTING THE STRIPS

Before you cut your bolt of wallcovering into strips for hanging, you should uncurl it so that it will lie flat. Unroll about three feet of the material and drag it firmly over the edge of a table to give it a reverse curl. Be careful not to crease the material. Repeat this step until the material lies flat. If the roll starts flat, you will not have to uncurl the whole roll.

Cut the first strip from the roll about four inches longer than the height of the wall. However, you cannot just cut similar lengths for the rest of the strips unless you have plain paper or a pattern that can be matched randomly. You must be sure that the second strip is long enough so that, if it must be raised or lowered to match the first strip, there is enough extra at top or bottom to cover the wall. If the pattern has a large vertical repeat so that there might have to be a large amount of waste material, you can sometimes cut down the waste by cutting alternate strips from different rolls; that is, cut the first, third, fifth strip, and so on from the first roll, and cut the even numbered strips from another. If you do this, you might want to number the back of the strips at the ceiling end so that you can keep track of the proper order of hanging them.

You should have a large table to work on, but if not, you can improvise by placing a wide plywood board five or six feet long on a bridge table. If you have a longer board, put it across two bridge tables for a firmer support. The width of the board or table should be at least double the width of a strip. Place the first strip on the table with pattern side up. Cut enough strips to do one wall, always making sure you leave a few inches extra at top and bottom and enough additional material to make sure the designs match from strip to strip. As each strip is cut, place it on top of the pile of strips with the pattern side up and all heading in the same direction. You will have to cut some short strips to go over doors and over and under windows. These short strips must be placed in the pile in the proper order. Now turn the whole pile over so that the top strip is the first to be hung, and all are in the proper sequence. Each strip will now have the pattern side down so that it is in the proper position for pasting. Push the whole pile to the back of the table.

8.7 HOW TO APPLY PASTE

Paste should be mixed from 15 to 30 minutes before it is to be applied. Mix the powder with water in a plastic paste bucket according to directions. Tie a string across the top of the bucket by punching holes near the top on opposite sides. You can then rest your brush on the string when you are not using it and thus keep the handle dry. When buying paste, make sure you buy the type recommended for the wallcovering you will use. After mixing the paste, spread newspapers on the floor near the walls and underneath and around your pasting table.

Pull the first strip off the pile to the front of the table, with the pattern still face down. Stretch the strip over the table so that its upper end, the ceiling end, hangs off the edge of the table. The bottom end of the strip should be on the table near the opposite edge. Start brushing the paste on from the bottom of the strip. When the strip is pasted over half its surface, fold the bottom edge over without creasing the paper so that pasted surface is against pasted surface. This is called *booking* and is shown in Fig. 8–6.

Slide the wallcovering along the table so that you can now apply paste to the rest of the strip. Leave the top inch or two unpasted. If the strip is very long, you may want to book the upper portion too, so that you can carry it without touching the floor. The strip is now

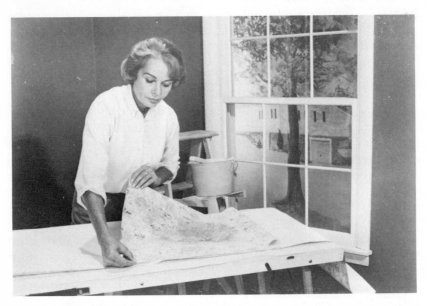

FIGURE 8–6. Booking. Photo Courtesy of Wallcovering Industry Bureau.

ready for hanging. Hang each strip before applying paste to the next one.

8.8 HANGING THE STRIPS

As you hang each strip, you must be careful to match the design to that on the strip preceding it. When you have gone around the room, it would be a rare coincidence if the pattern on the last strip matched the first. Since you must expect a discontinuity in the pattern, try to have the discontinuity where it will not be noticed. Thus, you would normally begin at the edge of a door and proceed around the room from there. Anyone entering through that door would have the discontinuity behind him and would be less likely to notice it. If there is a large window in the room you can let the window itself be the discontinuity in the pattern. Of course, if you are not hanging wall- covering on all walls, you do not have to worry about a mismatch where first and last strip meet.

The first strip must be hung exactly vertically. Do not depend on the walls or the edge of a door to be a true vertical, since houses are not built that exactly, and even if they were built to true verticals, there is always some sag and displacement. To locate the first strip, you must mark a true vertical on the wall. Do this before you apply paste to the first strip. Measure the width of the strip and then measure a distance one inch less than the width of the strip from the door or window where the first strip is to go. Drive a tack in the wall near the ceiling at this distance from the door. Attach your plumb line to the tack and rub the line with chalk. When the plumb line bob comes to rest, grasp it firmly without moving it and, with your other hand, snap the line against the wall, as shown in Fig. 8-7. You will now have a true vertical line on the wall. Every time you have to go around a corner, repeat the operation to get a new vertical reference on each wall.

Grasp the first strip near the top and climb up your stepladder. If the top was booked, unfold it. Hang the paper so that the top overlaps the ceiling joint by about two inches and so that one edge runs right along the vertical line, as shown in Fig. 8-8. Use a smoothing brush, not your hands, to rub the paper against the wall, as shown in Fig. 8-9. Use downward strokes of the brush and work from the center of the strip to the edges. When the top of the strip is smooth, unfold the bottom of the strip and smooth the rest of the strip to the wall.

After the bubbles have been smoothed out of the strip, cut off the excess at door edges, baseboards, and ceiling while the paper is still wet. The simplest way to do this is to use a wall scraper or putty

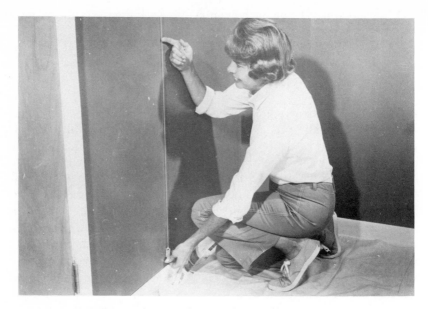

FIGURE 8–7. Vertical Line. Photo Courtesy of Wallcovering Industry Bureau.

FIGURE 8–8. Hanging the Strip. Photo Courtesy of Wallcovering Industry Bureau.

FIGURE 8-9. Smoothing. Photo Courtesy of Wallcovering Industry Bureau.

knife as a guide and cut the material with a sharp razor edge, as shown in Fig. 8-10. Before hanging the next strip, sponge off paste from baseboards, ceilings, and wallcovering, using clear water, as shown in Fig. 8-11. If the paste were to dry, it would be difficult to remove.

Hang each succeeding strip in the same manner, using the edge of the preceding strip as a guide. To move a strip, as for matching or lining up, place your palms lightly near the center and push up, down, or sideways as required. Do not grasp the strip at the edges to move it, or you will have paste on your hands and over everything.

Hanging paper behind a radiator may be a problem because you cannot get at the material with your smoothing brush. Use a long stick, such as a yardstick, with cloth wrapped around it. The same technique is used in any tight place.

Hang your wallcovering right over electrical outlets and switches after first removing the covers. When the paste is dry, cut away the paper around the opening. If there are wall brackets on the wall, they should be disconnected and removed before the wallcovering is hung. If this cannot be done, cut a slit in the material from the edge to the location of the wall bracket and slide each side of the slit under the bracket. Some additional trimming may be necessary, but you can paste all edges down so that the slit won't show.

Corners present some difficulty because they are not always square.

FIGURE 8–10. Trimming Excess. Photo Courtesy of Wallcovering Industry Bureau.

FIGURE 8–11. Sponging off Paste. Photo Courtesy of Wallcovering Industry Bureau.

When a strip is on one wall and part on the next, figure out approximately where the edge of the strip will be. Draw a vertical chalk line as a guide at that point. Now hang the strip, smoothing it carefully on the first wall and for about one inch of the second. Make sure it is snug in the corner. If the outside edge is not true with the chalk line, cut the strip about one inch from the corner and adjust it so that the edge is lined up with the vertical. There may be some overlap or mismatch at the corner, but it will not be noticeable. Whenever you go around a corner, set a new vertical reference line.

Hanging wallcoverings around windows or doors is not much different from the procedure on other walls. Line up the strip to match the preceding strip. With a scissors, make a diagonal snip in the strip at the corner of the frame. Fit the wallcovering in place and trim off the excess with a razor, using a scraper as a guide. This is shown in Fig. 8–12.

After strips have been in place for about fifteen minutes, roll the seams with the roller in your tool kit. In practice, you might roll the seams after hanging three or four strips. You must not roll the seams of flocked or embossed coverings, however, because you might crush them. For these papers, rub the seams lightly with a damp sponge.

FIGURE 8–12. Trimming Around Window. Photo Courtesy of Wallcovering Industry Bureau.

8.9 HANGING PRE-PASTED WALLCOVERING

If you are using pre-pasted coverings, you do not have to mix and apply paste, nor do you need a table. However, you do need a water tray. Otherwise, the procedure is similar to that for pasting and hanging.

Cut the pre-pasted strips in the manner described in Section 8.6. Reroll each strip loosely from bottom to top with the pattern inside. The strip is placed in the water tray next to the baseboard at the place where it is to be hung, as shown in Fig. 8–13. The water should be tepid. Follow the manufacturer's instructions as to temperature of the water and length of time to soak. Pull up the wallcovering from the water tray as shown in the figure and hang as described in Section 8.8.

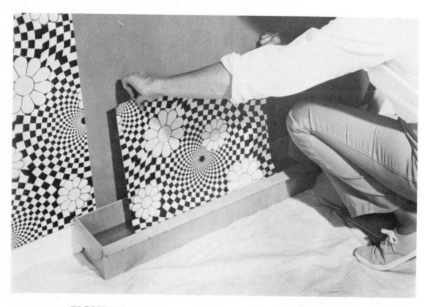

FIGURE 8–13. Pre-pasted Paper. Photo Courtesy of Wallcovering Industry Bureau.

III

Rigid Wallcoverings

9

Panels

Not too long ago, paneled walls were synonymous with luxury. The middle classes and poorer folk had to do with painted walls or wallpaper, but the very rich had wood on their walls. Panels ranged from formal, luxurious mahogany to informal, but still expensive, knotty pine. Each board was hand-cut and fitted into place, and this contributed to the expense. Today, new materials and simplifed installation techniques have reduced the cost of paneled walls so that this former luxury is now within the means of the masses.

9.1 MATERIALS

Instead of hand fitting individual boards, the handyman works with panels that cover large areas and are easily installed. Most panels are 4 feet wide and extend from floor to ceiling. A common size is 4 × 8 feet, but lengths of 7, 9, 10, 11, and 12 feet are also available. You can generally find a size that fits your walls so that sawing and trimming are minimized.

Hardboard panels are made of selected wood chips pressed together with a suitable binder to form a hard panel of the proper size. The hardboard is then coated with a synthetic finish that resembles wood grains, tile, leather, cork, marble, or almost any other material, as well as murals and a variety of original designs. The wood designs are realistic, representing vertical boards butted against one another. The "widths" of the boards, that is, the spacing between vertical grooves in the design, are random, as would be the case if individual boards were used. This also has an advantage that when one panel butts against another the line of demarcation looks like just another groove. Some designs of antique wood faithfully reproduce the worm holes in the wood as well as manufactured "defects" that one might expect to find in weathered wood.

Textured designs in hardboard panels look and feel like the authentic material. Simulated cracks in marble or old leather are there to touch as well as to look at. Other designs, such as abstracts, may be smooth or rough, according to the whim of the designer. Before choosing a material, look at samples of different panels from different manufacturers so that you cover a wide selection of types and styles.

Wood-veneered plywood panels start with plywood sheets of the proper size. The plywood is covered with a thin veneer of desired wood, and the finish not only resembles natural wood, it *is* the actual wood. In some of these panels, the wood veneer is impregnated with a transparent plastic so that it never needs maintenance. Even without the plastic, the wood veneer requires only the kind of maintenance used on fine furniture—an occasional dusting. The veneer is not an imitation. It is a thin layer of natural wood, showing grain, knotholes, and other "blemishes" in the original material. These blemishes are included to add interest, as accents, in what might be an otherwise monotonous expanse. This explains the attractiveness of knotty pine.

Wood-veneered panels come in natural wood colors and also may be stained with any of the usual wood stains. Hardboard panels with synthetic finishes can be manufactured in any color. Some are made in true natural colors, while other are in decorator colors.

When installing panels, especially if walls are not exactly vertical, you may find a gap at the top or bottom of a panel or at the junction of two panels or the junction of a panel and a door frame. To cover these gaps, and to dress up a paneling job, in general, manufacturers offer an assortment of moldings in colors to match the panels. The molding may be made of the same material as the panel or may be wood or aluminum covered with a veneer of matching material. Cross sections of some of the shapes are shown in Fig. 9–1. Others in the line include inside corners, spacers or dividers, chair rails, sills, and almost any other shape you might have to use to cover or hide an imperfection in the work. Each molding comes in lengths as long as the panels and is cut to size as needed for shorter runs. Some typical installations are shown in Fig. 9–2. In Fig. 9–2(a), a *base molding* is used to cover the gap between the bottom of a panel and the floor; a shoe molding is used to dress up the joint. In Fig. 9–2(b), a *cove molding* is used to cover the same sort of gap at ceiling level. When a panel is used to cover only part of a wall, the top edge of the panel looks unfinished. For the sake of appearance, a *cap molding* may be used to cover the edge, as shown in Fig. 9–2(c). When you are selecting panels, look over the wide selection of moldings available.

Panels and moldings can be attached with either special adhesives or finishing nails. Both are available from the manufacturer. Nails have heads that match the finish of the panel so that there is no need to countersink them. In addition, manufacturers supply putty sticks in colors to match the finishes of the panels. These may be used to touch up scratches and minor imperfections. The stick is simply rubbed

(a) Base   (b) Shoe   (c) Cove   (d) Cap   (e) Outside corner

FIGURE 9–1. Cross-section of Moldings.

over the scratch, and the spot is wiped with a dry cloth. The material dries hard quickly and hides the blemish completely.

9.2 DECIDING TO PANEL

There are many good reasons to consider paneling when a wall needs repair or refinishing, but your first reason must be that you like panels. If you don't like the look or feel of wood on the walls, there is no sense listening to a catalog of the advantages of paneling over other types of finish. Indeed, there is a place for paneling in every home, but also a need for other wall decorations.

If you are building a new room such as a basement playroom or converting a garage to a family room, paneling will save some work. Walls can be made of paneling fastened to the studs and will need no other finish. Another place where paneling may be indicated is in any room with severly damaged walls. Paneling can be installed right over cracks, holes, or other defects.

Paneling is relatively easy to apply. Complete installation instructions are presented in Chapter 10 and after reading them, you should be able to tackle the job with confidence that the result will be quite presentable. There is no messy cleanup procedure needed after the job is finished. If you saw panels indoors you will have to pick up the small amount of sawdust with your vacuum cleaner, but, aside from putting your tools away, that is all the cleaning necessary.

Paneling is no more expensive than other quality wall coverings. Cheaper hardboard panels are competitive with wallpaper. Wood-veneered panels are more expensive, but do not cost more than quality

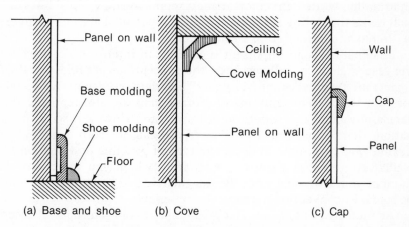

FIGURE 9-2. Molding Installations.

wallcoverings of other types. In panels, price does not depend on the type of wood or color, but rather on the method of fabrication. Many of the wood grains available in wood veneer are also available in hardboard, and the hardboard will pass all but the closest scrutiny.

As mentioned in the preceding section, panels are available in a variety of colors. Thus, paneling a room does not mean that it will necessarily be dark, although original wood panels were only of dark wood. You can have any color you need to blend with your furnishings. However, you would not want a solid unbroken stretch of four paneled walls in a room any more than you would want plain, painted walls. You should decide to add accents, perhaps by a combination of paneling and a patterned wallcovering.

One big advantage of paneling is ease of maintenance. Plastic-impregnated panels can withstand abuse and are easily cleaned of dirt, grease, and even wax crayons and ink. The finish lasts for years, literally as long as the wall lasts.

Paneling can be done piecemeal. You can panel one wall or even part of a wall, leaving the rest in wallpaper or paint. There's nothing wrong with a wood panel accenting a painted or patterned wall. Later, you can add additional panels, as you see fit, to make a solid paneled room or to leave a smaller amount of wallpaper showing so that the design becomes an accent in the paneled room.

9.3 HOW TO USE PANELING

The general principles of color harmony and design, explained in Chapter 7, apply equally to paneling. Dark colors make walls seem closer and smaller, while light colors make a room larger. Vertical lines on a wall make the ceiling seem higher. The apparent shape of a room can be altered by choice of color and design.

Imagination is an important ingredient in interior decorating. In the case of flexible wallcoverings, the conceptions of professional designers are reproduced, providing a rich variety of imaginative designs for your walls. The concepts of professionals are also reproduced in panels, although the variety is not as great. However, with imagination, there is no limit to the ways you can use both paneling and flexible wallcoverings. Indeed, the type of paneling or design on the wallcovering is just a starting point from which you can create the room of your own choosing. Be imaginative and inventive, and don't be bound by conventional uses of the materials.

As indicated in Chapter 7, a predominant color on the wall accentuates furnishings of the same color in the room. Going one step further, a material that predominates on the wall accentuates furnishings of similar materials in the room. This is shown in Fig. 9–3, where a knotty red cedar wood-veneered panel adds a touch of simple elegance to a wall and brings out the best qualities of the fine wooden furniture.

The treatment in Fig. 9–4 is somewhat different in that paneling is used on only one wall. Each large wood-veneered panel is "sculpted" so that it appears as an accent, adding to the quiet luxury of the room without monopolizing the decor. The result is a formal conversation area, but still warm and interesting.

An unconventional, but interesting arrangement of panels is shown in Fig. 9–5. Two different hardboard panels are used on the walls of this studio apartment. A rich looking rosewood panel is used in normal fashion in part of the apartment, and a white panel is mounted horizontally on another wall. In addition, painted hardboard is used on the ceiling to provide accents. Note how the horizontal paneling creates the illusion of a room separate from the rest of the apartment. For striking effects, panels can be used diagonally as well as horizontally. Lines on adjacent panels need not be in the same direction.

Paneling is most efficient when a new room is to be created. Two

FIGURE 9–3. Wood on Wood. Photo Courtesy of Georgia-Pacific Corporation.

FIGURE 9–4. Living Room Wall. Photo Courtesy of
Georgia-Pacific Corporation.

FIGURE 9–5. Studio Apartment. Photo Courtesy of
Masonite Corporation.

views of a recreation room built in a former garage are shown in Figs. 9-6 and 9-7. The hardboard shelving and paneling in Fig. 9-6 have a simulated brown oak finish that accentuates the color of the hexagonal coffee table. If the wall were bare, the wide expanse of oak paneling might be too monotonous. The painting on the wall in Fig. 9-7 breaks up the large area, but of equal importance is the fact that it ties the room together by featuring colors found in the rugs, drapes, and chairs.

Another newly created room is the laundry shown in Fig. 9-8. Here, the wood-veneered panel was chosen for its durability and imperviousness to water vapor. This simple paneling will probably outlast the laundry equipment. Note that in a work area such as this, you are usually more concerned with the practical attributes of the wallcovering than with its decorative value. No special care is taken to make the wall more interesting, although the contents of the horizontal shelf do break up the large uniform area of the wall.

The bathroom walls in Fig. 9-9 are also covered with wood-veneered panels that withstand water vapor. In contrast to the laundry and other work areas, lavatories should have interesting walls. The mirror,

FIGURE 9-6. Recreation Room Built in Garage. Photo Courtesy of Masonite Corporation.

FIGURE 9–7. Oak Wall with Painting. Photo Courtesy of Masonite Corporation.

FIGURE 9–8. Laundry. Photo Courtesy of Georgia-Pacific Corporation.

FIGURE 9–9. Bathroom. Photo Courtesy of
Georgia-Pacific Corporation.

painting, and towel ring and the contrasting patterns of the adjacent
wall furnish the needed accents.

Bathrooms conventionally have walls covered with tiles or marbleized plastic. Hardboard panels covered with tough plastic are available
to simulate tiles, solid colors, and other common bathroom walls.
The finish is heat-resistant and impervious to moisture so that these
panels can be used even around the tub and shower. A typical installation is shown in Fig. 9–10.

Dining rooms should be interesting but not exciting. A simple, but
formal treatment is shown in Fig. 9–11, where rough-textured white
hardboard paneling covers most of the wall area. Geometric patterns
add interest, but are not too stimulating for formal dining.

The decorations in a child's bedroom should grow up along with the
child. Since paneling lasts for years, it is important to choose a design
that will not be too childish when the child becomes a teenager or a
young adult. A boy's room designed to grow with the boy is shown in
Fig. 9–12. The wall is a rugged white hardboard, built to stand abuse.
As the boy grows, new decorations reflecting his new interests will
replace the old, but the wall is suitable for any age group. The storage
unit is also built of hardboard panels.

FIGURE 9–10. Marbleized Bathroom. Photo Courtesy of Masonite Corporation.

FIGURE 9–11. Dining Room. Photo Courtesy of Masonite Corporation.

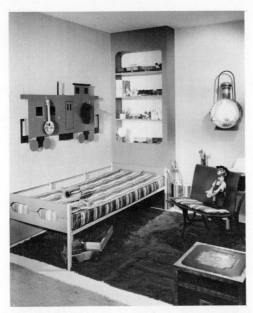

FIGURE 9–12. Boy's Bedroom. Photo Courtesy of Masonite Corporation.

The girl's bedroom shown in Fig. 9–13 illustrates an imaginative use of paneling beyond simple wall covering. The built-in canopy bed utilizes the same wood-veneered panels as the walls. Note that the panels that frame the canopy match the curvature of the panels that frame the bed. The pieces were cut from the same panel without waste. In this room, as in the boy's bedroom in Fig. 9–12, the walls will last throughout the girl's growing period and will be just as suitable for the teen miss as for the young girl.

An attic room with a sloping ceiling can present a decorating problem, but paneling can eliminate a major portion of the difficulty. The large attic room shown in Fig. 9–14 has a sloping ceiling at each end. The portion of the room under the sloping ceiling at one end was made into a walk-in closet with doors of the same woodgrain hardboard that was used on the walls of the room adjacent to that end. The textured white hardboard shown on the ceiling was carried over to the far wall (not shown) so that the room was effectively divided into two distinct areas.

Recreation rooms or playrooms are frequently paneled because they are additions, perhaps in a basement, and paneling is the most efficient method of combining construction and decoration. However, by proper choice of materials, you can make a recreation room as formal

FIGURE 9–13. Girl's Bedroom. Photo Courtesy of Georgia-Pacific Corporation.

FIGURE 9–14. Attic Room with Sloping Ceiling. Photo Courtesy of Masonite Corporation.

or informal as you like. The formal recreation room in Fig. 9–15 is designed as a showcase for the hobbies and interests of the occupants. White paneling on the walls creates the illusion of greater space and does not compete for attention with the collections. Rosewood hardboard provides a rich contrast, drawing attention to the individual collections separately.

An example of what can be done with a basement recreation room is shown in Fig. 9–16. A light-colored hardboard panel simulating antique wood was used on three walls and around the bar. Important considerations in choice of materials for recreation rooms are durability and low maintenance. One wall was covered with a bright plaid wallpaper to set apart a conversation area. Flooring is a brick-patterned, no-wax tile, again for ease in maintenance. To deaden noise, a shag carpet is used on the floor and a white acoustical tile on the ceiling.

When installing panels, you will have a certain amount of sawing to do, to fit pieces around doors and windows or to cut openings for ventilators and electric fixtures. Save all the odd scraps and use them for decorating other parts of the room, as shown in Fig. 9–17. The active areas in this recreation room are covered with a vinyl-covered, wood-veneered paneling that withstands abuse and needs no maintenance. One wall is painted a solid color and is accented with odd pieces of the same paneling.

FIGURE 9–15. Hobby Room. Photo Courtesy of Masonite Corporation.

FIGURE 9–16. Basement Recreation Room. Photo Courtesy of Masonite Corporation.

FIGURE 9–17. Recreation Room. Photo Courtesy of Georgia-Pacific Corporation.

10

How to
Install
Panels

The biggest problem in installing paneling is lack of confidence. Don't worry! The manufacturers have built the expertise into the product, including materials to correct errors. Read the instructions carefully and completely before you begin. You will see that there is nothing difficult about the installation.

10.1 ORDERING AND STORING PANELS

When you buy paneling, it is unlikely that you can make arrangements to return any unused panels for credit. Consequently, you must be able to make an accurate assessment of how many panels you will need. The "standard" panel size is 4 × 8 feet, and the "standard" wall is 8 feet high. Thus, a standard panel will reach floor to ceiling in an 8-foot room. If your ceiling is higher or lower, you can buy panels that are longer or shorter, but the cost per square foot for the 8-foot panels is lower than that for the others. If you are paneling less than the full height of the wall, use the height of the desired paneled section as the height of your room.

If you are paneling all the walls of a room, first measure the perimeter. This is the sum of the width of all four walls. If you are paneling only three walls, or parts of walls, then measure the width of the walls or sections you plan to cover. Divide the perimeter (in feet) or the width you will cover by 4. This will give you the number of panels that will cover the walls without regard to windows, doors, fireplaces, and other openings that would not be covered. Subtract one half of a panel for each door or fireplace and about one quarter of a panel for each window. These are approximations. If you wish, you can measure openings accurately. However, if you want to panel above and below windows and above doors, you should figure how these odd pieces can be cut from one panel. If you use approximations for openings you will probably arrive at the correct figure for the number of panels, but if your doors and windows are odd sizes, you should plan where each panel or piece of panel is to go and thus get an accurate figure for the number of panels needed.

When the panels arrive, store them in a dry place prior to installation. They should be stored flat to prevent warping. Panels may be shipped in large bags and packed in pairs with the faces of each pair toward each other and separated by a protective sheet. When removing the panels from the bags, slide them out two at a time, keeping the protective sheet between the adjacent faces so that the finish on each panel is protected. Separate the panels and stand them in the room where they will be installed. Leave them there for at least two days to become acclimated to the temperature and humidity in the room.

When you stand the panels in the room, you may notice differences in color, grain, or pattern of knotholes. You can arrange the panels around the room to get the most pleasing effect. When you have arrived at a suitable arrangement, number the backs of the panels in the sequence in which you plan to install them on the walls so that you can more easily keep track of them.

10.2 TOOLS NEEDED

No special tools are needed to install panels, but you should have a few common tools handy so that you don't have to look for them when you have to use them. You may not need all of those on the following list, but have them available:

Hammer

Nail set

Tape measure

Saw (hand or power)

Level

Small wooden block

Scraps of shingles or other wedge-shaped scraps

Caulking gun for adhesive (this is supplied with the adhesives)

Small compass for scribing

10.3 FASTENING METHODS

Panels can be fastened to the walls by nails or by adhesives. Each method has its advocates who claim it is superior to the other. Either method gives satisfactory results, but the two techniques are somewhat different.

When using nails for fastening the panels, you must first locate the studs in the wall. The nails are driven into the studs to furnish a sturdy support for the panels. Panels can be nailed directly over old wallpaper, on greasy or dirty walls, or on walls with gaping holes in them. Panels can also be nailed directly to studs in new construction where no wall existed before. One disadvantage is that each nail must be driven in separately with a hammer and nail set, and this may seem tedious.

When using adhesives, it is not necessary to know where the studs are, but the wall must be in suitable condition. You cannot use adhesive over wallpaper since the adhesive may loosen the wallpaper paste and pull the paper off the wall. Walls must be cleaned since the adhesive will not stick to grease or loose dirt. Adhesive can be used to stick panels to studs in new construction just as well as nails.

The supporters of adhesives claim it is faster and simpler than nailing. However, the total time for the job is more a function of experience than of your method of fastening. There is no doubt that nailing can be used in some situations where adhesives may prove unsatisfactory, but with proper care, both methods provide strong bonds to the wall.

10.4 INSTALLATION WITH NAILS

You can install panels from floor to ceiling or you can butt the panels against existing molding. If you elect to panel the whole wall, you must remove the old molding. Just pry it loose, and don't worry about damaging the walls because the paneling will cover any holes you make. In either case, measure the space where the panel is to go as accurately as possible. Due to the settling of the house, the height from floor to ceiling may vary around the room. Small differences are not important since gaps can be covered by moldings at floor and ceiling. The main reason for measuring is to trim the panels for installation where the ceiling is lower. The height of the panel should be ½ to 1½ inches less than the overall height to allow for expansion caused by moisture and temperature variations. Moldings will cover the gaps.

The panels will be nailed to the studs. In new construction, the studs are visible, and the panels are fastened directly to them. When remodeling, you must locate studs in the wall. When you tap lightly on the wall, you should hear a hollow sound between studs and a solid sound directly over a stud. You can also use an inexpensive stud locater. The studs should be spaced 16 inches apart between centers, and when you have found one, you simply measure at 16-inch intervals to locate the others. Drive a long nail lightly into the wall where you think a stud should be. If it goes in too easily, it is between studs, but if it encounters resistance, you've located a stud. Again, don't be concerned about nail holes or other defects since the new panels will cover them. Probe with the long nail on both sides of the stud until you have located it exactly. Draw a *vertical* line over each stud. The simplest way to do this is with a chalk line, as shown in Fig. 10–1, but you can use a yardstick and level to draw a vertical line on the wall.

Start in a corner and butt the first panel against the adjacent wall. The outer edge should fall on a stud and be parallel to the vertical lines. If the outer edge is not parallel, the intersection of the two walls is not exactly vertical. Shim the panel up from the floor by using wedges or scraps of shingles so that there is a gap of about half an inch at top and bottom. Make sure the outer edge is vertical, either by using a level or by checking it with the vertical lines you drew. If the gap at the wall is small at its widest part, you will be able to cover it with corner molding. However, if the discrepancy is more than about ¾ inch, you will have to trim the panel. Use the compass to scribe the amount to cut off. With the outside edge of the panel vertical and the panel touching the corner at one point, place the point of the compass against the adjacent wall, holding it in contact with the wall; draw a line on the panel from top to bottom. This is shown in Fig. 10–2. In addition to correcting for an irregularity at the corner, you may find it necessary to trim the panel so that the outer edge falls on a stud.

FIGURE 10–1. Drawing Line Over Stud. Photo Courtesy of Georgia-Pacific Corporation.

The panel can be cut with a handsaw or power saw. During the cutting stroke, the saw should enter the face of the panel, otherwise, it might split the veneer. When using a crosscut handsaw or table saw, have the panel face up, but with a sabre saw or portable power saw, it should be face down. Do not use a ripsaw. Both sides of the cut should be supported so that the panel will not split near the end of the cut. You can lay the panel on four sawhorses or on two bridge tables. Sawing a panel is illustrated in Fig. 10–3. When it is necessary to cut an opening in a panel, as for an electric outlet, first drill pilot holes at the corners of the opening. Then cut with a sabre saw or keyhole saw.

When the first panel is in its proper location, you should nail it in place. Start at the corners, as shown in Fig. 10–4. All nails should go into studs. For new construction with panels mounted directly to studs, use nails 1 to 1¼ inches long. Use the same length nails when nailing to furring (see Section 10.6). For application over old walls, use nails 1⅝ to 2 inches long. The edges of the panel should lie along studs, and nails should also be driven into the studs that lie between the edges. You can use ordinary finishing nails and countersink them. Then fill the holes with colored putty to match the finish on the pan-

FIGURE 10–2. Scribing at Corner. Photo Courtesy of Georgia-Pacific Corporation.

FIGURE 10–3. Sawing Panel.   **FIGURE 10–4.** Nailing.
Photos Courtesy of Georgia-Pacific Corporation.

els. This putty comes in stick form and can be purchased when you buy the panels. You can also use nails with colored heads that match the panels and eliminate the countersinking operation.

When panels are fastened directly to studs, nails should be spaced about 6 inches apart along the edges of the panels and about 12 inches apart elsewhere. Over furring, these spacings can be increased to 8 and 16 inches, respectively. Over old walls, space the nails 4 inches apart at the edges and about 6 inches elsewhere.

After nailing the first panel in place, butt the next panel up against it, using a wooden block at the edge to tap it up snugly against the first. As with the first, use wedges or pieces of shingle to keep the second panel about ½ inch off the floor. Nail this panel in place in the same manner as the first, and continue with the rest of the panels. Note that if you are paneling from an old molding instead of from the floor, the panels are butted right against the molding and are not shimmed.

After a few panels are up, you may come to a window or doorway less than four feet from the edge of the last panel. If, for example, only three feet of space remain, simply cut one foot off the width of the panel. Your saw cut doesn't even have to be straight because you can cover the joint with a molding. For the small space over the window or door, cut the proper filler from scrap pieces if possible. For example, after you trim the panel to fit into the 3-foot width, you will have a piece about 1 by 8 feet. Cut this into heights to fit over the door. For a fancier job, you can cut the panel to fit around the door as shown in Fig. 10–5.

When you come to the opposite corner, you may be lucky and find that the space from the edge of the last panel to the corner is exactly 4 feet and about ½ an inch. (You should leave about ¼ to ½ inch of space to take care of possible expansion of the panels.) More likely, you will have to cut a panel to fit, just as for the door mentioned in the preceding paragraph. Cut the piece and nail it in the same way that you nail a whole panel. Now when you start on the next wall, begin flush with the corner. The first panel on the next wall will hide any irregularities in your saw cut. If you wish, you can cover the corner with molding to hide the joint completely. This is shown in Fig. 10–6.

10.5 INSTALLATION WITH ADHESIVES

Adhesives can be used to fasten panels on new studs, on furring, or on painted walls. The wall should be clean. Adhesives should not be used over wallpaper or on walls that are crumbling. Since the posi-

FIGURE 10–5. Door Cut-out. Photo Courtesy of Georgia-Pacific Corporation.

FIGURE 10–6. Corner Molding. Photo
Courtesy of Georgia-Pacific Corporation.

tion of the studs with respect to the panels is immaterial, you do not
have to locate the studs as you do for nailing, but the rest of the installation is similar.

Panel adhesives come with a caulking gun. Place the tube of adhesive in the gun and cut off the tip of the spout on the tube. With a
long nail, puncture the seal at the bottom of the spout, and the gun is
ready to use. To operate, pull the trigger with the spout next to the
wall and squeeze the adhesive out like toothpaste from a tube. One
tube could last for five panels if used sparingly. But it is better to use
it generously and expect to put up only three panels with each tube of
adhesive.

Fit the first panel in place in a corner, making sure the outer edge
is vertical. Use a level or plumb bob to make sure the edge is correctly
aligned. If necessary, trim the inner edge to fit in the corner using the
compass to determine the proper amount of trim, as shown in Fig. 10-2.
Have someone else hold the panel in place or, if no one else is available, wedge the panel in place with scraps of shingles. Then draw a
vertical line on the wall next to the outer edge of the panel. Take down
the panel and apply adhesive in a continuous line ½ inch inside the
perimeter of the whole panel, all the way around. Now add horizontal

dabs of adhesive on the area inside the perimeter. These dabs should be about 3 inches long, and spaced about 6 inches apart horizontally and 16 inches vertically. Now press the panel in place. Make sure the outside edge is vertical and allow at least ¼ inch at top and bottom for expansion. (If you have left the old base molding in, you can butt the bottom of the panel against it.)

Pound the panel against the wall to squash the adhesive. You can use your fist or a hammer on a cloth-covered block. Now pull the upper part of the panel from the wall, leaving the bottom edge touching, and rest the panel against the back of a chair. Allow the adhesive to set for about ten minutes and then push the panel back against the wall, again making sure the outside edge is vertical. Pound the panel again and press it firmly in place. Now you're ready for the next panel.

The rest of the installation is the same as for nailing. Doorways and corners are treated as described in the preceding section. Moldings are *nailed* in place after the job is finished.

10.6 FURRING

If your old wall has bulges in it so that the paneling will not lie flat, or if you wish to panel over masonry walls, you will have to use furring strips. These are simply pieces of 1×2 inch lumber nailed to the wall to provide a flat surface for supporting the panels. Horizontal strips are fastened along the whole width of the wall with a 16-inch vertical spacing between centers. Then, short vertical strips are added with a horizontal spacing of 48 inches between centers. The arrangement is shown in Fig. 10–7.

On plaster walls, the horizontal furring strips cross the studs, and the shorter vertical strips lie right on the studs. All the strips are nailed to the studs. The nailheads should be below the surface so that they won't interfere with the paneling. On masonry walls, use masonry nails to fasten the strips. If the original wall is uneven, use shims under the furring so that the surface of the strip is vertical. You can check this with a level.

After the strips are in place, you can install the panels either by nailing or using adhesives. If you use nails, they should be placed in all horizontal strips. Adhesive is applied to all the strips with the same spacing as is used for a plain wall.

10.7 ELECTRIC BOXES

If an electric outlet, switch, or fixture lies on the area to be paneled, you will have to cut a hole in the panel to accommodate it. For an out-

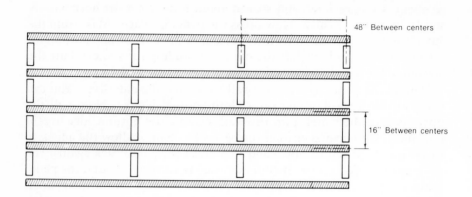

FIGURE 10–7. Furring Strips.

let or switch, simply locate the position on the panel and draw an outline of the box. Drill pilot holes at all corners and cut out the material with a keyhole saw or sabre saw. Don't fret if your saw cuts are crooked, since the wall plate overlaps the edges. However, you will have to pull the outlet from the level of the old wall to the level of the new panel. Longer screws in the junction box will be required.

For a light fixture, you will have to disconnect the wires. Cut a round hole in the proper place in the panel using a sabre saw or keyhole saw with a diameter smaller than the diameter of the fixture. After the panel is in place, connect the wires again and replace the fixture. Whenever you work near electric wires, make sure the electricity is disconnected.

10.8 CARE AND MAINTENANCE

Panels can usually be cleaned with just a damp cloth. If necessary, use a mild soap or detergent to remove crayon marks and other stains. Do not use abrasive cleaners, as these may mar the finish. The surface may also be lightly waxed.

Although panels are unusually tough and wear-resistant, they can be abused. Light scratches can be removed by rubbing on a clear wax with the grain. Deeper scratches can be touched up with putty that matches the finish. This is usually available in stick form from the dealer who supplies the panels.

11

Masonry
Panels

Brick and stone have unusual beauty and charm and lend an air of elegance to a room. From a practical standpoint, a brick fireplace or a stone wall requires no maintenance. Masonry panels are now available to enable the home handyman to install his own brick or stone with very little effort and no prior experience.

11.1 MATERIALS AND DESIGNS

Masonry panels are made of crushed limestone reinforced with fiberglass. Real stone gives the panels an authentic texture, while the fiberglass provides strength and durability. A close-up view of a wall covered with man-made masonry paneling is shown in Fig. 11-1. Even an expert could be fooled into believing the wall is made of genuine bricks. An additional advantage: the masonry panels are hollow, and the dead air space provides good thermal insulation. The panels are much more inexpensive than real bricks.

Masonry panels weigh about one pound per square foot. This is heavier than wooden panels, but much less than the equivalent area of

FIGURE 11-1. Close-up of Brick Wall. Photo Courtesy of Masonite Corporation.

Masonry Panels

real brick or stone. Masonite Corporation manufactures three different types. Their *Heritage* series reproduces weathered bricks, arranged 12 to a panel, as shown in Fig. 11-2. The staggered bricks permit inter-locking adjacent panels during installation. Their *Carriage* series have 24 bricks to a panel and look and feel like new sculptured bricks. The arrangement is shown in Fig. 11-3. Both of these series are available in white, buff, and light or dark red. Masonite's *Bedford* series repro-duces the beauty of natural stone in a panel 1 × 4 feet in area. The panel looks like a section of wall made of stones of random sizes, as shown in Fig. 11-4. Bedford panels are available in white, grey, and buff.

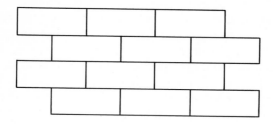

FIGURE 11-2. "Heritage" Panel by Masonite.

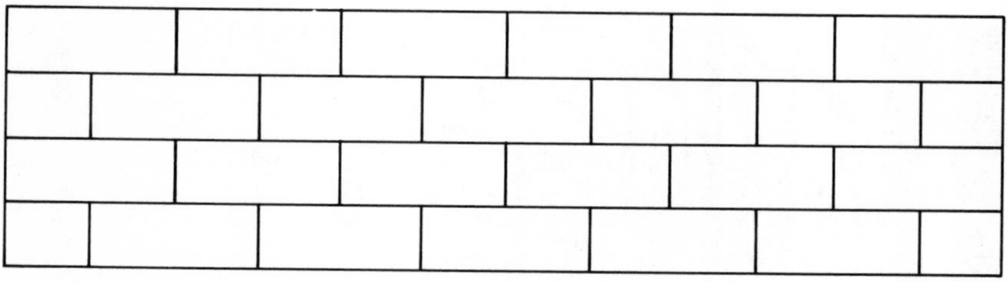

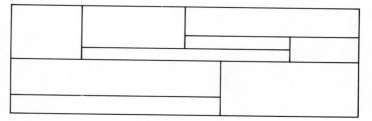

FIGURE 11-3. "Carriage" Panel by Masonite.

FIGURE 11-4. "Bedford" Panel by Masonite.

Masonry panels can be used in any room of the house. You wouldn't want all four walls in a room to be an endless expanse of stones or brick, but a suitable combination of a brick wall or section with paneled or papered walls in the rest of the room can be an unusual and elegant touch. The brick paneled wall in the entryway in Fig. 11-5 is inviting and friendly and looks like real brick. A natural place to use masonry panels is in a playroom, as shown in Fig. 11-6. The warmth and beauty of natural stone add a touch of excitement to the room. The luxurious bathroom in Fig. 11-7 features a red brick sitting area and an ornate black grill doorway leading to the dressing room. The brick is made of masonry panels, and the grill is a decorator panel. The bath area is framed in stucco, which is made of hardboard panels with a stucco surface. Masonry panels can also be used around a fire-place, behind a counter in a kitchen, or on one wall of a dining room. They blend well with either formal or informal decorations, but always add an aura of luxury.

The three types of panels shown in Figs. 11-2, 11-3, and 11-4 are all designed so that adjacent panels interlock for ease of installation. The staggered end bricks in Fig. 11-2 provide an obvious and simple

FIGURE 11-5. Entryway with Brick Wall.
Photo Courtesy of Masonite Corporation.

FIGURE 11–6. Natural Stone Paneling. Photo Courtesy of Masonite Corporation.

FIGURE 11–7. Bathroom with Masonry Wall. Photo Courtesy of Masonite Corporation.

method of interlocking panels horizontally. The Carriage panels of Fig. 11-3 interlock vertically by means of a flange arrangement shown in Fig. 11-8. The upper panel has a groove in its bottom edge into which the tongue of the lower panel fits. Note that the fastener for the lower panel is then completely hidden by the upper panel. The stone panels of Fig. 11-4 have an overlapping joint, as shown in Fig. 11-9. Both panels have lips that are overlapped during installation, and

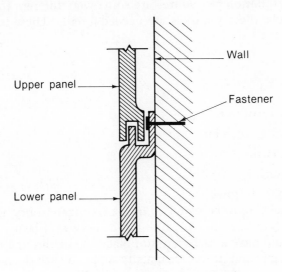

FIGURE 11-8. Interlocking Panels.

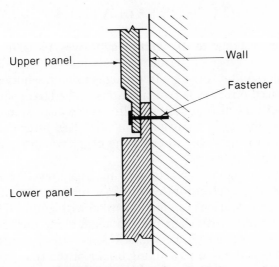

FIGURE 11-9. Overlapping Joint.

fasteners are driven through both at once. The fasteners are located in the mortar lines of the stones and are subsequently covered with grout or mortar.

11.2 TOOLS NEEDED

Although installation procedures are somewhat different for the three types of panels, the same tools are needed for all. These tools should be available:

Hammer

Nail set

Level

Tape measure or ruler

Drill with 3/16-inch bit

Hacksaw or sabre saw

Caulking gun

3/8-inch margin trowel

If the panels are to be installed over existing masonry, the drill bit should have a carbide tip. Any fine-toothed saw may be used, but preferably it should have a carborundum blade to cut through the panels. The caulking gun and trowel are usually supplied with the mortar.

11.3 INSTALLATION

Panels may be fastened to the wall by adhesives, nails, or special fasteners. All three types of masonry panels may be installed on solid walls or on horizontal furring. If furring is used, the horizontal strips should be spaced 6 inches between centers. The larger panels of Figs. 11-3 and 11-4 may also be fastened directly to open studs. The Heritage panels of Fig. 11-2 are usually installed beginning at the top and working down to the floor, whereas the other two are installed from the floor level up to the ceiling.

To install Heritage panels, begin by placing a level horizontal line 11¼ inches from the ceiling or the top of the installation. If the ceiling is not level, any deviations can later be filled with grout. The first row of panels is installed with their bottom edges along the line. Start at one corner and work across the wall. If you start at an inside corner, you must saw off the two protruding bricks of the first panel. If you start at an outside corner, you should purchase *outside corners*, which are made to cover a corner and interlock with panels on both adjacent walls. If only one wall is to be covered, cut off the two overlapping bricks and fill in the openings. To do this, stuff paper into the openings and finish with mortar. When this dries, it may be colored with special touch-up material to match the brick.

Special nylon fasteners are used to hold the panels, as shown in Fig. 11–10. A 3/16-inch hole is drilled through the mortar line and wall. Then the fastener is inserted in the hole and the nail is driven flush with a nail set, as shown in Fig. 11–11. As each panel is installed, two fasteners are inserted to hold it. These fasteners are positioned as shown by the letter X in Fig. 11–12. When the next adjacent panel is installed, additional fasteners are inserted in the common junctions, as shown by the circles in Fig. 11–12. If the wall itself has sufficient holding power, you can use screws or nails instead of the nylon fasteners. If adhesive is used instead of fasteners, a continuous bead of adhesive is placed along the back of each mortar line.

Panels in successive rows are brought into light contact with those above them. When you come to the floor, it is unlikely that you will have an exact fit and it will be necessary to trim the bottom panels to fit. Use a saw to cut the bottom panels or plan to install a base molding to hide the gaps. Fitting at windows or around trim is also accomplished by cutting. Edges can be filled with mortar.

After the panels are installed, grout or mortar is applied with a caulking gun, as shown in Fig. 11–13. The mortar covers both the nylon fasteners and the seams between adjacent panels. The caulking gun is held at a 45 degree angle, and a slight pressure is applied to make

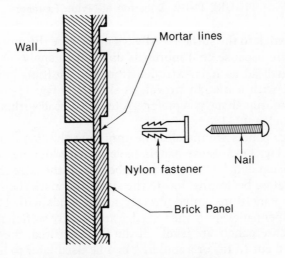

FIGURE 11–10. Nylon Fasteners.

FIGURE 11–11. Installing Fasteners. Photo Courtesy of Masonite Corporation.

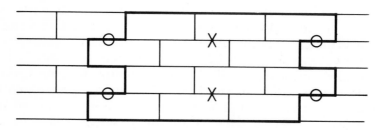

FIGURE 11–12. Location of Nylon Fasteners.

the grout stick to the surface. Always make sure the mortar is at room temperature because cold mortar is difficult to apply. You can leave the mortar bead as it is extruded from the caulking gun or you can smooth it with a margin trowel, as shown in Fig. 11–14, to achieve whatever mortar shape you prefer. A finished bead without smoothing is shown in Fig. 11–15.

Carriage panels are installed beginning at the floor. Although not shown in Fig. 11–3, these panels have an interlocking strip that protrudes at each end. This strip must be cut off the edge that fits into a corner. Before beginning, locate the studs and mark their locations on the wall. Panels are nailed directly to the studs with 1½-inch nails. Four nails per panel along the top edge are usually sufficient.

Make sure panels are level. If the floor is tilted, the panel can be scribed and cut to fit, or a molding can be used later to cover the gap. If the floor is level, a starting strip may be used first at floor level.

FIGURE 11–13. Applying Mortar. Photo Courtesy of Masonite Corporation.

FIGURE 11–14. Smoothing Mortar. Photo Courtesy of Masonite Corporation.

The first panel locks into the starting strip and is thus held firmly at the bottom. Four nails hold the top firmly. These nails are hidden by the next panel, as shown in Fig. 11–8. If no starting strip is used, the lowest panels should be nailed to the studs at the bottom as well as at the top. Drill holes in a mortar line near the bottom to accommodate the nails. These nailheads can be touched up later.

FIGURE 11-15. Finished Mortar Joints. Photo Courtesy of Masonite Corporation.

As each new row of panels is begun, make sure vertical mortar lines are staggered for best visual effect. Each panel is interlocked with the one below, as shown in Fig. 11-8. When you get to the top, you will probably have to trim the top panel to fit. Then drill holes for nails and nail the top panels to the studs. Touch up the nails later. If a space is left at the top, it can be filled with mortar.

Around windows and doors, there are three options. You can use wood moldings as you would with wood panels. Since the door frames are wooden, these moldings would not look out of place. Stone moldings to match the panels are also available. The third choice is to fill the space with mortar and color it to match the brick. Stone and brick moldings are also available as a cap for wainscotting.

Bedford panels are also installed from the floor up and are nailed directly to studs. Stud locations should be marked on the walls. Start at a corner and make sure the panel is level. Any space at the floor can be covered with a base molding. This is simpler than trimming the panel to fit. As with Carriage panels, mortar lines should be staggered.

When all the panels are in place, mortar is applied to cover all nailheads and to fill any cracks and openings. Also, all the recessed mortar joints between the panels are filled. The mortar should be smoothed with a margin trowel up to one hour after it is applied. Mortar sets to a waterproof seal in about two days.

11.4 SMALL OPENINGS

Before the panel is installed over a small opening such as an electrical outlet, mark the location on the wall, as shown in Fig. 11-16. Then fit the panel to place and mark the panel for cutting around the opening, as shown in Fig. 11-17. Cut the panel and nail it in place. Remove the outlet box and reset it with longer screws so that the wallplate can be set over the brick or stone.

11.5 MAINTENANCE

Masonry panels need no protective maintenance. Dirt and grease can be removed with water and ordinary household detergents.

FIGURE 11-16. Locating Electrical Opening. **FIGURE 11-17.** Marking Panel for Opening.

Photos Courtesy of Masonite Corporation.

Index